Ancient Cities of the Southwest

ANCIENT CITIES

Chronicle Books · San Francisco

of the SOUTHWEST

A Practical Guide to the Major Prehistoric Ruins

of Arizona, New Mexico, Utah, and Colorado

Text and photographs by Buddy Mays

Foreword by Joseph C. Rumberg, Jr.
Former Director, Southwest Region, National Park Service

Library of Congress Cataloging in Publication Data:
Mays, Buddy.
Ancient cities of the Southwest.
Includes index.
1. Cities and towns, Ruined, extinct, etc.— Southwest, New—Guide-books. 2. Indians of North America—Southwest, New— Antiquities—Guide-books. 3. Southwest, New—Antiquities—Guide-books. 4. Southwest, New—Description and travel —1981– —Guide-books. I. Title.
E78.S7M356   917.9'0433   81-21732
ISBN 0-87701-696-8   AACR2

Illustrations:
Reproductions of pre-Columbian rock art on pages 35, 38, 46, 53, 67, 71, and 113 are from Rock Art of the American Indian, *copyright ©1967 by Campbell Grant, published by Thomas Y. Crowell Company. Reproductions of pottery designs on pages 1, 3, 15, and 24 are from* Art of a Vanished Race: The Mimbres Classic Black-on-White *by Victor M. Giammattei, D.V.M., and Nanci Greer Reichert, copyright ©1975 by Dillon-Tyler, Publishers. Reproduced by permission. Illustrations on pages 69, 87, 88, 91, 93, 103, 111, 117, and 118 are by Howard Jacobsen.*

3 4 5 6 7 8 9 10

Book design:
Howard Jacobsen

Editing:
Carey Charlesworth and Philip C. Johnson

Composition:
TBD Typography

Chronicle Books
275 Fifth Street
San Francisco, California 94103

Contents

FOREWORD 8

PREFACE 11

ACKNOWLEDGMENTS 14

INTRODUCTION 17

EXPLORING FROM PHOENIX, ARIZONA 25

1 Pueblo Grande Ruin (Phoenix Municipal Monument) 27

2 Montezuma Castle National Monument 29

3 Tonto National Monument 33

4 Casa Grande Ruins National Monument 37

EXPLORING FROM FLAGSTAFF, ARIZONA 39

5 Walnut Canyon National Monument 41

6 Tuzigoot National Monument 43

7 Wupatki National Monument 45

EXPLORING FROM KAYENTA, ARIZONA 47

8 Navajo National Monument 49

9 Rainbow Bridge Trail 53

EXPLORING FROM BLUFF, UTAH 57

10 Monument Valley Navajo Tribal Park 59

11 Hovenweep National Monument 63

12 Natural Bridges National Monument, White Canyon 67

13 Grand Gulch Primitive Area   71
14 Comb Wash   *75*

EXPLORING FROM CORTEZ, COLORADO   77

---

15 Salmon Ruins (San Juan County Research Center)   79
16 Aztec Ruins National Monument   81
17 Mesa Verde National Park   83
18 Ute Mountain Tribal Park, Mancos Canyon   87

EXPLORING FROM GALLUP, NEW MEXICO   *89*

---

19 Canyon de Chelly National Monument   91
20 Chaco Culture National Historical Park   95

EXPLORING FROM ALBUQUERQUE, NEW MEXICO   *99*

---

21 Salinas National Monument   101
22 Coronado State Monument, Kuaua Pueblo   105

EXPLORING FROM SANTA FE, NEW MEXICO   *107*

---

23 Pecos National Monument   109
24 Bandelier National Monument   113
25 Puye Cliff Dwellings   117

EXPLORING FROM LAS CRUCES, NEW MEXICO   *119*

---

26 Gila Cliff Dwellings National Monument   121

DIRECTORY OF SITE HEADQUARTERS   123
GLOSSARY   125
FOR FURTHER READING   128
INDEX   130

Foreword

WHEN I was growing up in southwestern Colorado in the 1930s, my father owned and operated a small sawmill. Every summer during my school years I worked in the woods and in the mill as a regular hand. The mill was situated on Lost Canyon, a tributary of the Dolores River, and any free time I had I spent exploring. This entire region was once home to a people we have since named the Anasazi. The remnants of their settlements can still be found in the remote mesas and canyons, and you can imagine my surprise and pleasure when I found, tucked under a section of sandstone cliff, just such a place.

By today's standards it wouldn't draw much attention, but to a young lad exploring, it was a rare find. Sandstone block walls, ridgepoles, and a smoke-blackened cave ceiling made the picture complete. Even someone's initials and discovery date carved on a ridgepole didn't detract from my delight for long. The little ruin was just under the rim at the top of the canyon with a good southern exposure, no doubt for heat from the sun during the cold winter months, and an excellent view of the La Plata Mountains. It was a prime homesite even by today's standards. I spent many happy hours daydreaming in and around that ancient homesite, speculating about who had lived there, where they had come from, where they went, and why. Oddly enough, almost half a century later, I find that our knowledge of the Anasazi can answer only some of these basic questions.

Following my tour of duty with the Marines in the South Pacific, I started working in Mesa Verde as a seasonal ranger in summers while I attended college. Jack Wade, the Chief Ranger, was a nephew of Richard Wetherill who figured prominently in the early discovery and exploration of many cliff dwellings, including Cliff Palace in Mesa Verde. Jack had grown up on the Navajo Reservation working for his uncles and had been on various horseback parties in which his uncles acted as guides. His firsthand knowledge of ruins such as Betatakin, Keet Seel, Canyon de Chelly, and Chaco Canyon served to whet my appetite. In the mid-1940s there were no roads to speak of in the Navajo country, only two tracks through the sand that forked and reforked without benefit of signs. Nevertheless, I made some unforgettable trips with Jack, and visiting some of those historic remnants in those years was a difficult and wonderful accomplishment.

On my first visit to Navajo National Monument with Jack, the trader at Shonto (a Navajo trading post near Navajo National Monument) was "Shine" Smith, an old friend of Jack's. He told us of a squaw dance being held that night just east of the trading post. There were wagons and horses by the dozen but only one other automobile. Altogether there were only five non-Navajos at the ceremony. At that time, particularly on the west side of the reservation, the Navajos still wore the traditional long hair tied in a braid in back. Practically none spoke anything other than his native tongue. Imagine such a setting, with a full moon just beginning to rise in the east, countless small campfires, and the smell of sagebrush smoke. On the far side of the sage-brush flat, the drums began and high falsetto voices started the chants. To me it was like traveling back to a distant time. I found the hair on the back of my neck beginning to rise. Here I was experiencing part of an ancient healing rite with the knowledge that around us were the even more ancient, silent cities that had once been occupied by those the Navajos call the Anasazi, the "Ancient Ones."

Such experiences are what give me a rather special feeling about those people who were, together with their ancestors, truly the first Americans. During my National Park Service career, I was fortunate to serve in many fine areas of the system. Even in the areas that were set aside for their natural beauty, geological significance, or purely recreational values, one could always find evidence of earlier occupants whose footsteps preceded ours by hundreds and sometimes thousands of years. Let us hope we never become so blasé, so insensitive, that we fail to feel a kinship, a sense of reaching across time to touch and thereby form the bond so necessary to give us consciousness of place and being.

My early years and associations in Mesa Verde did much to prepare me for successively more responsible positions in the National Park Service. It also helped me to understand man's place and his relationship to other men. I love to recall the story of the early archaeologist in Mesa Verde who was working in a ruin across the canyon from Balcony House. He sincerely believed that he heard the voice of an Anasazi speaking to him. Can you doubt him? I don't, for I've stood in the vacant rooms of the Ancient Ones and have felt their presence.

Use this comprehensive guide to find, visit, and explore not only those ancient homesites protected by the National Park Service, but also those located on other properties and worthy of your time and interest. The guide provides an excellent thumbnail sketch of each area as well as travel directions. The introduction gives you a very good background; the only ingredient lacking is your desire, so go stand in a room of the Ancient Ones, maybe they will talk to you.

JOSEPH C. RUMBURG, JR.
Former Director, Southwest Region
National Park Service
U.S. Department of the Interior

Preface

I FOUND my first arrowhead when I was nine—a leaf-shaped, nearly perfect flint point lying in soft, sandy mulch beneath a rose bush in my front yard. Needle-sharp, about an inch long, and colored a deep red, it was probably lost by some buckskin-clad hunter a thousand years before (or so I liked to think). I'd never found one before, but as I rubbed it between my thumb and first finger, I knew immediately what it was. I knew simply by the feel. Here was a piece of the man-made past.

That was the beginning. Ever since, off and on, I've pondered the when, why, and how of prehistoric Americans. Believe me, pondering enigmas wasn't easy for a nine-year-old, and frankly it hasn't gotten any easier 28 years later. To ponder properly requires a certain amount of factual material. Archaeological fact, friends, is evasive. The main fact of archaeology (in fact) is that no one, Ph.D. or S.A.L. (Smart Alecky Layman) knows beyond the shadow of a doubt what was happening way back then during the gestation of human knowledge. Therein lies a problem; if no one knows for sure, the only way to approximate understanding is to guess, and guesses are sometimes inaccurate. Often inaccurate. Many in fact are so far off target they wouldn't qualify as near misses in a spitball-shooting contest between Snow White and a one-eyed salamander.

Guessing, however, is one of archaeology's necessary evils. The Introduction and the rest of this book therefore demand a little explanation. In an effort to paint a logical and understandable portrait of the three major periods of prehistoric human occupation in the Southwest—Paleo-Indian, Archaic, and Pithouse-Pueblo—I found that a certain amount of guesswork was unavoidable. Readily, I admit my personal knowledge of archaeology is limited. Although I can easily differentiate between a sherd of polychrome pottery and the left front fender of a 1959 Nash Rambler, right there is where fact stops and guessing begins. Who made that sherd? Woman, man, boy, girl—I don't have the faintest. Was he or she short, tall, fat, skinny, light, dark, bald, hairy? Likewise, I can only guess; that's all anyone can do.

However, as my research progressed and I sorted my guesses into a semblance of order, I requested input from others, mainly "experts" in the field of archaeology. Naively I believed that their guesses would be similar to mine, and that, from the acquired data, I could form some logical, if unprovable, conclusions. I drew up a list of relevant questions concerning primitive man in the Southwest, then contacted several qualified people. Came a rude awakening; with the exception of a few universally accepted archaeological tenets, no one's guesses agreed with mine. Not only did the archaeologists disagree with me, they disagreed with each other. To a man (and woman).

Let me cite an example. A minor subscience of archaeology is the study of coprolites—fossil excrement, including that of humans. Most field scientists have a working background in coprology because analysis of human feces, petrified or otherwise, quite often gives clues as to composition of primitive diets. My question, dealing indirectly with coprology, was this: How did cliff-dwelling Indians conduct their sanitary needs in order to protect themselves and their fellow cliff-house residents from potential disease?

"On the ground," one archaeologist told me.

"On the ground *where*?" I wanted to know. "Do you mean that in the middle of the night, dark as sin, here comes this Anasazi climbing down his cliff to find a bush and . . ."

He smiled knowingly. "Maybe they had flashlights," he concluded.

"By exercising physical restraint," another said. "Over eons of adaptive ecological experience, aboriginal inhabitants structured their sanitary necessities and requirements to fit an infallible regimen until proper locale was available."

I had to think about that one for a while. I'm still not sure what he meant. Frankly, I'm not even sure he knew what he meant.

Like batwings on a night wind, other scientists whispered their conclusions softly, perhaps fearful of contradiction. "Everywhere." "Anywhere." "Almost anywhere." "They certainly did," and so on. I found one expert up in Utah who casually mentioned that the Anasazi and most other early cultures were excellent and prolific potters. "You ever heard of a chamber pot?" he asked. "Fill it up during the night, empty it in the morning? Potters—potties? Ha ha ha ha."

As it turns out, to some extent they were each correct. Waste removal, as I came to discover, varied from cliff dwelling to cliff dwelling. In some ruins, coprolites have been found everywhere—outside the front door, inside the front door, in the firepits, even on the roof. In others, no coprolites have been found at all, suggesting those particular Indians were somewhat more fastidious.

Which brings me to the point of this entire soliloquy. In trying to formulate my portrait, I amassed in my notebook enough guesses and narrow opinions to fill an Anasazi chamber pot several times over. Therefore, choosing those I assume to be the most reasonable, and without attempting to explain the hundreds of esoteric descriptions, categories, groupings, and subgroupings formulated by generations of archaeologists, anthropologists, sociologists, and biologists, I have put together what I hope is an understandable glimpse at probable human evolvement and habitation in the American Southwest from 25,000 B.C. until the Historic Period began in the mid-sixteenth century. This piece of advice I offer, however. When you consider Indian prehistory, begin each sentence with "maybe," end it with "probably." And if your guesses don't agree with mine, I won't be surprised.

Acknowledgments *I greatly appreciate the assistance given me by the National Park Service in the preparation of this book, especially that offered by Ben Moffett and Cecilia Matic of the Office of Public Affairs for the Southwest Region. I would also like to thank Gene and Mary Foushee, Marie-Claude Wrenn, and Barbara-Ellen Koch for their assistance in gathering and compiling research material and photographs. Finally, a great many thanks to archaeologist James Lancaster and several dozen overworked National Park Service rangers who argued me out of numerous blunders.*

Ancient Cities of the Southwest

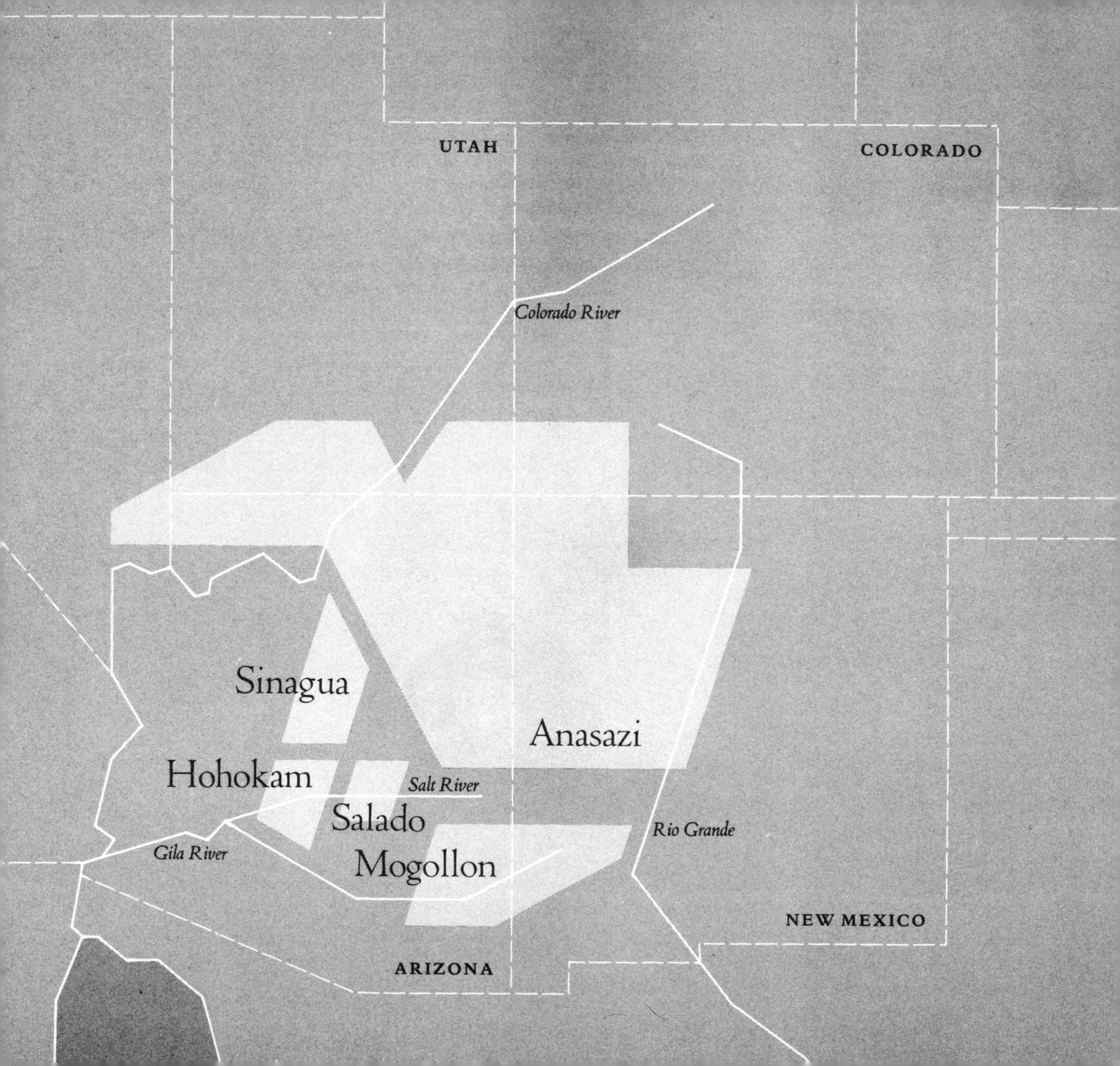

UTAH   COLORADO

Colorado River

Sinagua

Anasazi

Hohokam

Salt River

Salado

Gila River

Mogollon

Rio Grande

NEW MEXICO

ARIZONA

Introduction

MOST archaeologists agree that *Homo sapiens* did not originate in North America but migrated here from Asia sometime during the final stages of the Pleistocene Epoch, a dramatic period in earth's history that most of us know as the Ice Age. During the Pleistocene, nearly one-sixth of the earth's surface was blanketed with ice; it was ice, in fact, that made man's arrival in North America possible. As massive glaciers formed from billions of tons of water, oceans receded; in some areas sea level dropped as much as three hundred feet. In consequence, long-submerged fragments of sea bottom were exposed, and one of these—a 56-mile–long strip of rocky earth between northeastern Siberia and northwestern Alaska—was early man's gateway to this continent.

Exact dates of man's New World penetration are simply unobtainable with present technology. Giving ourselves a margin for error, however, we can say that aboriginal Asian man probably arrived upon North American shores about 25,000 B.C. That, of course, is give or take a few millenia. His arrival was not sudden. Late in the Pleistocene, interglacial subages (warming trends) began to occur, causing sea-level ice to melt. As the climate slowly mellowed, grass and low shrubs flourished, even on the newly exposed land bridge. This forage attracted grazing animals from the Asian continent, which in turn attracted the attention of hunting man. Following the mammoth and bison, he came, pursuing the herds from one land mass to another without knowing he did so.

Since a people dependent upon stealth and patience for food cannot survive in large numbers, early American man probably moved in small clans; when game became scarce in one area, the hunter had little choice but to move to another. Both man and beast followed the ice-free corridors that had opened southward because of the warming climate. Their migration could not have been easy in the heavily forested, subarctic wastes of Pleistocene Alaska, but nonetheless, through hundreds of generations, hunter and hunted worked their way south. So began the Paleo-Indian Period in North America.

When did man first reach the Southwest? No one knows. Archaeological evidence—mostly the dateable artifacts found with bones of extinct animals—suggests, however, that he was firmly entrenched in relatively large numbers by 10,000 or 12,000 B.C. Two extremely important finds supporting this theory were made in New Mexico in the early part of this century. In 1926, scientists examining fossilized bones unearthed near the small town of Folsom discovered several flint projectile points imbedded in the skeletons. The animals were identified as *Bison antiquus figginsi,* an early form of buffalo known to be extinct for at least seven thousand years. Radiocarbon dating suggested the creatures had been killed nine thousand to ten thousand years ago. A few years after that discovery, in the nearby town of Clovis, New Mexico, more flint points were uncovered—these with the bones of bison and mammoth. Radiocarbon analysis suggested these weapons were at least twelve thousand years old.

Since these two original discoveries, thousands of similar sites have been examined, and, through painstaking study, scientists have reached some logical conclusions. (1) Paleo-Indians were primarily meat eaters; although they are assumed to have gathered wild plants for food, no evidence of that exists. (2) Using flint- or bone-tipped weapons of their own creation and design, Paleo-Indians could and did kill animals 20 times their size. (3) At least in part, early man was a social creature; he hunted in well-organized groups so as to kill not a single animal but an entire herd at one time for the good of the clan or community. (4) Because constant expansion of hunting range was necessary, fixed habitations were seldom constructed. Paleo-Indians probably lived in caves. Admittedly, not a great deal of knowledge exists about a race of people that blanketed a section of North America for several thousand years. It is, however, all we have.

By 7000 B.C., human lifestyles in the Southwest were changing significantly, the modifications so noticeable that modern scientists distinguish a separate cultural stage for this more technologically advanced *Homo sapiens.* From about 7000 B.C. until the time of Christ, man was creeping from his shell. This span of cultural amplification has been named the Desert Archaic Period. Among the most important changes to occur during the Archaic Period were these: (1) the acquisition of the fire-drill and the grinding stone; (2) utilization of foods other than meat—mainly seeds, wild grains, tubers, and berries; (3) construction of semipermanent, seasonal habitations—primarily round or rectangular holes in the earth covered with brush and mud ("pithouses," which were developed extremely late in the Archaic Period); and (4) the practice of rudimentary spiritual ceremonies.

It must be understood that the span of the Desert Archaic Period is loosely defined; cultural advancement did not occur at exactly the same moment among all the inhabitants of the Southwest. The development of the Paleo-Indian into the Archaic Indian was a sluggish process at best, dependent upon interaction between groups of people sometimes separated by hundreds of miles. This was not so of the next period of cultural expansion—the Pithouse-Pueblo Period—which began shortly after the time of Christ and ended with the arrival of Europeans in the Southwest in the mid-sixteenth century. If man had crept from his shell before, he was now free and running.

Of the many changes occurring during the fifteen-hundred-year–long Pithouse-Pueblo Period, none exceeded in importance, and indeed all were connected to, the development of widespread, separate, and distinguishable human societies. By A.D. 700, five distinct groups of people had evolved and were inhabiting the Southwest. In the northern part of their area, scattered across a vast region of high desert known today as the Four Corners area (where the borders of Colorado, Utah, Arizona, and New Mexico meet), were the Anasazi—an intelligent, artistic, peaceful society of farmers whose cliff palaces and sprawling canyon-bottom cities were so well constructed that many have survived almost unblemished for a thousand years. (The earliest Anasazi, those who lived between A.D. 200 and 700, are called the Basketmakers because of the splendid wicker baskets they made; the Anasazi who lived between 700 and 1300 are called Pueblo Indians because of their early acquisition of above-ground building techniques.) To the south, near the San Francisco Peaks area of present-day Arizona, were the Sinagua, an agricultural people whose culture later became a melting pot of building techniques and sociological enlightenment. In the Gila and Salt River valleys near present-day Phoenix, Arizona, were the Hohokam, at their peak perhaps the greatest canal builders in North America. To the east were Hohokam cousins, the Salado; and in the rich mountain country of present-day New Mexico, the Mogollon.

How and why did these divisions of culture come about? What combination of circumstances nudged small clusters of seminomadic individuals toward more complex and structured societies? We can only guess. One probably important factor was the introduction and development of agriculture—a totally new concept to primitive man. Because agricultural products could be stored for the winter, dependence upon hunting and gathering was drastically reduced. In turn, habitations became more permanent so that farmers could tend their fields. Permanency demanded security from enemies; security required a large and stable population.

Whatever the reason or combination of reasons, these five major cultures (and many minor ones) arose. Geographically they were separated by hundreds of miles, and in many ways—especially in language—they were different. Yet each bore striking similarities to the others as well. For instance, they were all agricultural societies, heavily dependent for survival upon crops of maize (corn), beans, squash, and melons. In their early stages of development, all lived underground or in caves, later moving to above-ground, apartment-style, multistoried homes. By A.D. 700, all used pottery extensively and had acquired the bow and arrow. Three centuries later, cotton and the implements with which to weave were also in use. More important, as far as archaeologists can determine, none of these early cultures cultivated nor tolerated an aristocracy, such as was common in both the Aztec and Inca civilizations to the south. Prehistoric political structures in the Southwest were probably democratic in nature: Members of the community or clan appointed a leader to coordinate community affairs for the benefit of all. If he didn't do his job, he was replaced.

Similarities among the cultures occurred also in their people's physical appearance, clothing, and daily activities. From examination of mummified remains and other burial evidence, scientists think that most prehistoric Indians were about the same size and build; men averaged five feet, four inches, the women slightly less. They were muscular, stocky people with sparse body hair. Head hair was thick, however. Men usually wore it long; women preferred it bobbed or fashioned into elaborate coiffures.

Clothing varied, but variations depended less upon location than upon the time of year. In hot weather, most Indians wore nothing but sandals woven from plant fiber or plaited from yucca leaves. As the seasons changed and the days cooled, skirts and aprons made from vegetable material or animal skins were added. In winter, hide cloaks, shirts, and blankets—the latter made from rabbit skin, dog fur, or turkey feathers—were probably sufficient to turn the chill. When cotton was introduced and Indians learned the art of weaving, more elaborate forms of winter clothing—mainly heavy cloaks—came into vogue.

These similarities were not by coincidence, of course. Throughout the 15-century span of the Pithouse-Pueblo Period, interaction undoubtedly occurred among all prehistoric cultures in the Southwest as well as in northern Mexico, with each contributing something to the cultural pot. The Anasazi, for instance, were perhaps the instigators or at least the advocates of above-ground construction; the Mogollon used pottery and the bow and arrow first, then passed on their new-found knowledge directly or indirectly, on purpose or not, to their neighbors. The Hohokam and Salado were the most productive farmers and probably contributed the practice of irrigation; the Sinagua, centrally located between the northern and southern cultures, perhaps acted unknowingly as publicity agents for these new methods.

The Mexican Indians played an extremely important role in this cultural enlightenment. It was they who introduced corn to their northern neighbors, though exactly when this occurred is anyone's guess. It could have been as early as 2000 B.C. or as late as the time of Christ; whenever, the arrival of this particular agricultural product in the Southwest was probably the single most important event in the prehistory of the American Indian. The Indians of northern Mexico additionally brought the first metal (copper) into the Southwest; and they introduced what today we could call "frivolities." In this period the Hohokam and Sinagua began to play a type of body ball, the object of which was to knock a gum sphere through wooden rings at either end of an elaborate court. The game was probably an early form of *poc-ta-poc*, a sport still in evidence in Mexico today. The Anasazi played a form of dice, using bone game pieces marked with paint or tree pitch; although no definite proof exists, this pastime, too, probably originated in Mexico.

So rapidly did new ideas and methods spread among the five major cultures of the Southwest that, by the mid-eleventh century, they had developed a golden age of the Pithouse-Pueblo Period. Contributing to the new prosperity, increased rainfall had mellowed the sometimes harsh environment; natural springs and streams ran full, and game and wild plants flourished. Because of the added moisture and new agricultural techniques, farming increased, too; and with surplus food available, populations grew. New farming projects were started in areas that a century before hardly could have supported cactus. Existing towns and fields grew larger and more complex.

This new life of relative comfort was only temporary, however, and although many explanations as to why the golden age was suddenly cut short are plausible, one of the most feasible is this: By the middle of the twelfth century, cyclic weather patterns had once again changed, and the region saw the beginning of drought conditions. In areas where water was permanently available, farmers were little affected; in others, especially in communities where agriculture depended upon rainfall, existence once again became difficult. Many towns and outlying family dwellings were abandoned, the inhabitants migrating to larger centers of population that had been constructed near natural groundwater sources. What possessions could be carried were taken along; all else was left behind.

As the migrants quickly discovered, however, the land surrounding permanent sources of water was already taken. This sudden increase in refugees must certainly have created hardships for the already settled populations. Nonetheless, in most cases room was found. Dwellings were enlarged, and, where possible, new fields planted. As an additional measure, several of the especially large communities such as Chaco Canyon initiated systems of "outliers"—smaller communities built (or enlarged) near rivers or springs to furnish the main town with agricultural products and services in exchange for protection.

But then a new threat appeared in the Southwest. Shoshonean raiders (probably the ancestors of present-day Utes) suddenly arrived uninvited from the north, and local Indians found themselves the targets of continual harassment. Few in number, the Shoshone dared not attack a fully protected town, but they easily raided fields, stole harvests, and picked off an occasional farmer or his family. In addition, towns and villages had begun, probably out of necessity, to prey upon themselves. One clan with less food or land than a neighboring group likely thought little of taking what it needed—by stealth or by force. The Indians developed enemies without, and within, too.

Sometime during the late twelfth century, the combination of harassment, thievery, and steadily worsening drought conditions brought about a drastic change in lifestyles for most of the Southwestern cultures. The people began to leave their traditional valley or mesa-top homes for the security of isolated caves and protected canyon amphitheaters. Some towns had been constructed in caves originally and were simply fortified; others possessed good water sources and populations large enough to protect both fields and farmers, and these communities went unchanged. Thousands of the not-so-fortunate moved, however—lock, stock, and turkey. Interestingly enough, early in the drought some clans had reconnoitered possible future homesites with just such a move in mind, sending a few families to literally hold the fort until such time as it was needed. The time arrived, and the Indians moved—escaping into regions so inaccessible that even today they are seldom visited by man.

Whether the move actually ended the Shoshone threat or only prolonged it, we don't know. It did little, however, to ease internal strife or to alleviate the need for water. In the mid and late 1200s, even as the great cliff cities of Mesa Verde, Mancos Canyon, Betatakin, Keet Seel, and others like them were under construction, the drought was reaching its peak. Even permanent water sources began to go dry, and life became a matter of day-to-day survival. The soil was worn out, and it turned to dust; crops failed year after year. Hunting and gathering had never been fully abandoned, but wild food supplies decreased in direct proportion to the decrease in moisture. There was simply not enough food and water for the population. The very young and very old were probably the first to suffer, but as conditions worsened, none were left unaffected. Although we have no idea of its exact nature, some type of social upheaval undoubtedly took place—perhaps a universal uprising against blameless but available leadership. Migrations began. By 1299 when the drought finally ended most villages and towns of the Anasazi and Mogollon had been abandoned. Hohokam, Salado, and Sinagua communities (most of them near permanent streams) survived longer; however, they met the same fate within a century.

It is here that the real mystery begins. Where did the refugees go? Some probably journeyed east to join or found pueblos on the Rio Grande River in present-day New Mexico. Others went east but not as far, stopping at the pueblos of Zuni and Acoma, also in New Mexico. Some may have gone south to Mexico or west to California, and a good many simply changed their lifestyles to meet current requirements for survival and remained nearby, the ancestors of today's Pima and Hopi.

The Hopi mesas, in fact, were perhaps a major refuge for both the Sinagua and Anasazi. Hopi people claim ancestral ownership of many of the great population centers—Mesa Verde, Betatakin, Keet Seel, and Wupatki included. Prehistoric Hopi clan signs found in these ruins give validity to the claims, though many archaeologists argue the point, applying the old riddle: Which came first, the Hopi or the sign? Pictographs (prehistoric rock paintings) and petroglyphs (prehistoric rock carvings) similar to those the Hopi claim as clan symbols were once freely used throughout both North and South America. This certainly suggests widespread interaction among early cultures but not necessarily the traditional ownership of the signs that Hopi legends proclaim. Hopi ancestors were probably an aggregation of several different cultures.

Wherever the people went, they were gone, for the most part, by A.D. 1400. (Although several Anasazi communities in New Mexico were occupied until the 1500s, the later residents were probably migrants from other, more western communities.) They abandoned to the wind the homes so painstakingly constructed. Many of these prehistoric dwellings, preserved by dry desert air, and in some cases by the stabilization and restoration technology of modern science, still exist; the best of these I have described in this book. Of course, thousands and probably hundreds of thousands of prehistoric dwellings are scattered throughout the American Southwest. Many, however, are decayed beyond recognition by wind and weather. Others, intact though they may be now, face destruction because of careless human visitors. The Federal Antiquities Act specifies huge fines for vandalism, but archaeological treasures have been stolen, walls have been trampled, buildings marked indelibly with human graffiti—all because of the lack of a human trait, consideration. Consequently, those sites that scientists consider in "critical" condition are not included here, and only those dwellings that are in some way protected by federal, state, or local agencies have been described. When visiting these ancient ruins, remember that you are walking upon a short but important piece of the earth's history. Take nothing when you leave but knowledge, and leave nothing that was not already there. Allow those who come after you the privilege of viewing that history unmarred.

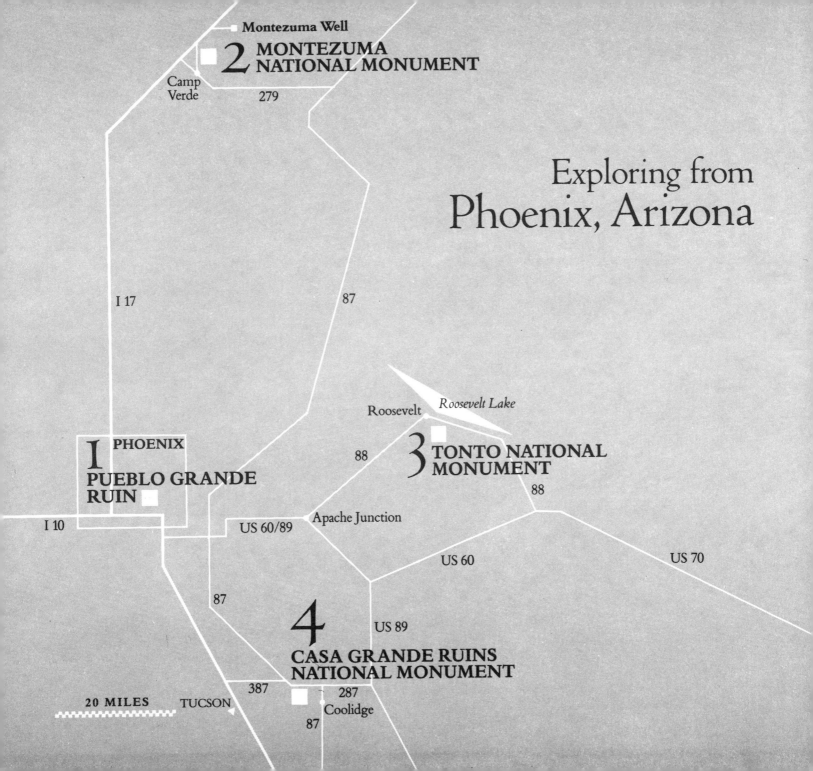

Montezuma Well

2 MONTEZUMA NATIONAL MONUMENT

Camp
Verde

279

Exploring from
Phoenix, Arizona

I 17

87

Roosevelt   *Roosevelt Lake*

1 PHOENIX

PUEBLO GRANDE RUIN

88

3 TONTO NATIONAL MONUMENT

88

I 10

US 60/89   Apache Junction

US 60   US 70

87

4

US 89

CASA GRANDE RUINS NATIONAL MONUMENT

20 MILES   TUCSON

387   287
Coolidge

87

I

Pueblo Grande Ruin
(Phoenix Municipal Monument)

HOHOKAM

HOURS   Weekdays and Saturdays, 9
A.M. – 4:45 P.M. Sunday, 1 P.M. –
4:45 P.M.

ELEVATION   1140 feet.

ACRES   83.

LOCATION   Urban Phoenix: 4619 E.
Washington Street.

ACCESS   The ruins are reached by a
short, self-guiding trail beginning at
the Pueblo Grande Museum.

FACILITIES   Drinking water and
restrooms are available at the
museum. Camping is prohibited,
but the site has a small picnic area.

INTERPRETIVE SERVICES   Advance
reservations are required for guided
tours. Trail-guide leaflets, available
at the information desk, give most
of the known information about the
ruin. A fine museum contains large
exhibits of Hohokam artifacts,
burial displays, and reconstructions
of Hohokam life. From June
through August, visitors can watch
archaeological digs in progress.

*Crumbling house walls at Pueblo
Grande Ruin. Burial remains found at
the site (inset).*

THE Pueblo Grande Ruin is a partially excavated, unrestored pueblo-style village built atop a large, man-made earth mound. Most of the dwellings are made of hard caliche mud and granite blocks; the site is surrounded by a defensive mud wall. Construction on this small pueblo was begun by the Hohokam people about A.D. 700. The Hohokam were farmers, descendants of a seminomadic Desert Archaic people who occupied the territory now called Arizona as early as 8000 B.C. Here they carefully tended large fields of maize (corn), beans, squash, cotton, and probably tobacco, irrigating their crops by means of an extensive system of canals that transported water from the nearby Salt River.

For several centuries the Pueblo Grande Hohokam probably resided in relative comfort. By A.D. 1300, however, life had become more difficult. After centuries of excessive irrigation, the fields were salt encrusted and water-logged; they would no longer produce enough food. Worse, Shoshone raiders from the north found preying upon the peaceful Hohokam farmers relatively easy. A slow exodus began, perhaps to friendly villages in the Gila Valley to the south. By 1400, Pueblo Grande had been totally abandoned.

The first non-Indian visits to the ruin took place in the 1860s, when settlers migrated to the Salt River Valley in search of fertile land. In 1924 the site was donated to the city of Phoenix; archaeological excavations began shortly thereafter and continue today.

Sections of the Hohokam canal system can still be seen near the ruin (though most of it has been destroyed by urban sprawl). At the peak of its expansion, the canal system was the largest irrigation complex in prehistoric North America and one of the largest in the world.

Some of the dwellings here are built atop "platform mounds"—man-made hills of earth and rock. Perfectly usable lower rooms were filled with this debris, plastered over with mud, and then smaller dwellings were built on top. The reason for such construction is unknown. It was perhaps a defensive measure to elevate village warriors above their attackers.

2 Montezuma Castle National Monument

SINAGUA

HOURS Summer, 7 A.M. – 7 P.M. daily. Winter, 8 A.M. – 5 P.M. daily.

ELEVATION 3200 feet.

ACRES 842.

LOCATION Central Arizona, 95 miles north of Phoenix on Interstate 17. The exit is well marked. A detached portion of the monument—Montezuma Well—is 11 miles northeast of the Castle, also on Interstate 17.

ACCESS A self-guiding, .3-mile loop trail beginning at the Visitor's Center leads to the base of the limestone cliff in which the Castle was constructed. Because of the ruins' fragility, however, access to the Castle itself is prohibited.

A loop trail to Montezuma Well, 11 miles from the Castle, begins at a National Park Service hut near the parking area. This trail, too, is self-guiding and about .3 mile in length.

Montezuma Castle, which was at one time thought to have been built by Aztec refugees.

MONTEZUMA Castle is a striking, five-story cliff house of about 20 rooms, built in a shallow limestone cave a hundred feet above the floor of Beaver Creek Canyon. This narrow chasm slices through the northern edge of the Lower Sonoran Desert. The dwelling walls are of rough, chunked limestone, laid together with pulverized-clay mortar and plastered with mud. The Castle is one of the best preserved of southwestern cliff dwellings and looks today much the same as it did during its fourteenth-century occupation.

North of the main monument is Montezuma Well, a 470-foot–deep water source in limestone that pumps 1.5 million gallons of water each day into Beaver Creek. Around the well's rim are several cliff dwellings and at least one unexcavated pueblo.

By A.D. 700, the part of Arizona we know today as the Verde Valley was occupied by Hohokam farmers. Several clans resided near Montezuma Well, living in above-ground pueblo-style houses near the rim and utilizing the well's continuous, substantial water supply to irrigate fields of squash, beans, corn, and cotton.

In 1065, a massive volcanic explosion occurred near the San Francisco Peaks to the north. That area was then occupied by another prehistoric group, the Sinagua. Like their neighbors to the south, the Sinagua were basically farmers. Their particular style of agriculture, however, depended upon rain for moisture instead of irrigation.

In the years following the eruption, Sinagua farmers discovered that the layer of volcanic ash covering the land increased farming productivity dramatically; and less than a century later, the region was suffering from overpopulation. So many farmers were working the land, in fact, that even with the help of volcanic ash the soil was quickly becoming infertile.

About 1125, small groups of Sinagua moved south into the Verde Valley, there to join the Hohokam. As the years passed, the Sinagua adopted the practices of irrigation and, instead of pithouse construction, above-ground

FACILITIES Drinking water, restrooms, and public telephones are
available and books are for sale at
monument headquarters. Both the
ruins trail and monument headquarters have wheelchair access. A
well-shaded picnic area is situated
adjacent to Beaver Creek beneath a
large grove of sycamore trees.
Camping is not allowed.

INTERPRETIVE SERVICES No guided
hikes are offered; trail-guide leaflets
are available at the Visitor's Center
for both castle and well. A small
exhibit center displays examples of
Sinagua pottery, handicrafts, and
other artifacts.

building techniques; and that was when the first rooms were constructed in
the great limestone cave overlooking Beaver Creek, which today we call Montezuma Castle.

Less than a century passed before drought conditions in the north sent
thousands more Sinagua people fleeing to their relatives in the Verde Valley.
Suddenly, even the spacious valley was overpopulated; farmland was the subject of heavy competition. The sociological and ecological balance of the
region was so disrupted by the influx of new arrivals that friction among
families, clans, and towns was inevitable. Perhaps they preyed upon each other
when food was in short supply; perhaps they fought over religious differences.
Perhaps, too, outside influences—such as fierce Shoshone nomads—added to
the discord.

Possibly because of a need for privacy, but more likely for security,
more rooms were added to Montezuma Castle; and by 1300 the cliff dwelling
was occupied by about 50 people and was the center of a large Sinagua community that occupied the canyon below. However, the strife must have
·become unbearable; by 1400, Castle, well, and the entire countryside had been
abandoned. Believing in greener pastures, no doubt, most of the valley's occupants probably moved south to join Hohokam villages in the Gila Valley.

The first visit to Montezuma Well by Europeans took place in 1583
when Spanish explorer Antonio de Espejo rode through the region. The
Castle, however, lay undisturbed then, and was first visited by U.S. Army
personnel in the 1860s. Even as late as 1884, only superficial examination had
been made of the dwellings. The name Montezuma Castle originated with
Verde Valley settlers who thought the cliff house had been constructed by
Aztec refugees fleeing from the Spanish conquest of Mexico. Official monument status was bestowed in 1906.

Of particular note at the monument are the Castle's tiny doors; some
early visitors assumed the cliff dwelling had been built by pigmies. But though
the Sinagua were small—averaging five feet, four inches—they were hardly
pigmies. Small doors kept out cold in the winter and extreme heat in the summer. They also could have made necessary head-first entry (as did T- and
P-shaped doorways). For an attacker to enter head first was not an exceptionally brilliant idea when mama was waiting inside with club in hand.

The Castle ceilings have no smoke-holes—a condition that must have
caused a considerable problem during cold weather, when cooking was done
inside. Campfire smoke collecting in the rooms probably created a dark,

foggy, and somewhat unhealthy interior. The Surgeon General, of course, had not yet issued his warning.

Another unusual feature is that Montezuma Well, though icy cold and replete with edible plant species, is totally devoid of fish because the water has an extremely high CO_2 content. The great well is still considered sacred ground by some Arizona Indian tribes.

Small cliff houses beneath the lip of Montezuma Well.

3 Tonto National Monument

HOURS   8 A.M. – 5 P.M. daily. Visitors must begin on the ruins trail by 4 P.M.

ELEVATION   2805–3150 feet.

ACRES   1128.

LOCATION   East-central Arizona; take U.S. 60/89 east to Apache Junction and turn left on Arizona 88. Stay on 88 through the town of Roosevelt. The monument entrance is 3 miles south of town on the right. *Caution: 25 miles of Arizona 88 is unpaved and mountainous and may wash out in wet weather.*

ACCESS   A steep, self-guiding trail leads to the Lower Ruin; the round trip is .8 mile. The Upper Ruin round trip is about 3 miles; for it, reservations are required (see below). During the summer, carry plenty of drinking water.

Lower Ruin at Tonto.

THE Tonto National Monument comprises two similar but separate cliff dwellings nestled in shallow caves, in the canyon country of the lower Sonoran Desert. The Upper Ruin contains about 40 rooms, the Lower Ruin about 20. (These ruins are in separate canyons.) The walls of both dwellings are constructed of unshaped quartzite stone and adobe mud. Several rooms in the Lower Ruin have been restored to their probable original state.

The Salado culture originated in the Little Colorado River drainage several hundred miles to the north, and moved into the Tonto Basin area of what is now east-central Arizona sometime between A.D. 900 and 1000.

The Salado were a peaceful people, building compact but unprotected villages in the canyon bottoms of the basin, close to their fields of corn, pumpkin, cotton, beans, and squash. Salado artisans were talented and prolific, especially in the arts of pottery making and weaving.

Sometime during the mid-thirteenth century, the peaceful life of these shy agriculturalists underwent a dramatic transformation. Perhaps because of raiders or the fear of them, the Salado people abandoned their canyon-bottom villages and constructed new homes on the upper canyon rims and ridge tops of nearby desert mountains. Fifty years later they moved once again, this time into mountainside caves. What thing or circumstance drove them into hiding is unknown. Still, life went on. Farming continued in the valleys below even though it required a 10-mile walk each day to the fields.

Soon after 1400, the Salado moved again. Cliff villages were abandoned, fields left untended. This time, however, the people simply disappeared. Archaeologists think they may have migrated east to New Mexico, perhaps to join the great river pueblos along the Rio Grande.

For several centuries the cliff dwellings lay undisturbed; then, in the 1870s, they were discovered by ranch cowboys. To protect the buildings from destruction by treasure hunters, they were given official monument status in 1907.

Drinking water, restrooms, and a soft drink machine (the most popular facility at Tonto) are available and books are sold at monument headquarters. A shaded picnic area is next to the Visitor's Center. No camping is allowed at the monument, but plenty of sites are available at nearby Roosevelt Lake.

INTERPRETIVE SERVICES   A visit to the Upper Ruin, where you must be accompanied by a ranger, requires a five-day advance reservation. Tours begin at 9 A.M. and are given only four days a week. Call to learn which days (see Directory). For the Lower Ruin, trail-guide leaflets are available in the Visitor's Center; they are keyed to numbered stakes along the route. Also, an exhibit hall contains a small display of Salado artifacts, and a 16-minute introductory slide presentation describes the ethnobotany of the region.

The Salado are especially noteworthy for their use of natural dyes and wooden loom tools such as spinning sticks and spindle whorls. With these Salado weavers created elaborate cotton cloth, which was fashioned mainly into shirts. A breech cloth, sandals, and a rabbit-fur blanket completed a typical Salado male's wardrobe.

Half-T- or P-shaped doorways at the Tonto ruins, like full-T doorways in many Anasazi dwellings, have mystified generations of doorway specialists. Many archaeologists say the unusual openings had religious significance; perhaps, but two simple advantages could account for their use. The shaped doorway would have regulated the temperature within if, during the winter, the upper half of the T or P were blocked by a shaped stone to conserve heat while the narrow bottom was left open for ventilation. In the summer, removing the stone could have allowed air to circulate through the room. Yet the enlarged upper half of the doorway would have allowed people (even pregnant women) to enter with large water jars or bundles of firewood in their arms, and without bumping their elbows. In addition, a T or P shape restricted attackers to entry one at a time—head first and ready for the club.

Ruins at Tonto National Monument sit in a Sonoran Desert landscape.

4 Casa Grande Ruins National Monument

HOHOKAM

HOURS 7 A.M. – 6 P.M. daily.

ELEVATION 1400 feet.

ACRES 472.

LOCATION Fifty-four miles southeast of Phoenix. Take Interstate 10 south to the Arizona 387 exit. Leaving the freeway, drive east to the junction of Arizona 87. The monument entrance is on the right, just past the junction.

ACCESS The main ruins complex is reached by a paved, four-hundred-yard trail that begins at the Visitor's Center. The unexcavated Indian mounds are not open to the public.

FACILITIES Restrooms and drinking water are available and books are for sale at monument headquarters. A shaded picnic area is just north of the parking lot. Camping is not allowed.

Casa Grande—"The Big House."

SCATTERED about an area the size of three city blocks and surrounded by saguaro cactus and a forest of creosote is the Hohokam town of Casa Grande. It is made up of 60 or so eroded dwellings, several unexcavated mounds, and the remnants of a seven-foot–high encircling wall. The centerpiece of the ruins is a mysterious thick-walled, four-storied structure built of unreinforced caliche mud, which rises from the town's heart. The building was not used as a dwelling, and archaeologists have no idea of its original purpose. This unusual structure gives Casa Grande ("Big House") its name.

Ancestors of the Hohokam—people of the Desert Archaic culture—occupied the present site of Casa Grande as early as 1300 B.C. Not until A.D. 1350, however, did construction begin on the walled town we see today.

Like their relatives at Pueblo Grande, 50 miles to the north, Casa Grande's inhabitants were farmers and maintained an extensive system of canals from which to irrigate their crops of corn, beans, cotton, and tobacco. Excellent craftsman resided here as well, skilled especially in the arts of stone sculpture and pottery making. Some artisans used a form of vegetable acid to engrave elaborate designs on seashell pendants. Others worked with copper, which suggests at least intermittent trade relations with Mexico since the art of metal refining was not acquired in the Southwest until after the arrival of Spanish explorers in 1540.

Casa Grande was not abandoned until about 1450, far later than most other Indian towns in the Southwest. Perhaps, because of the nearby Gila River, the people here suffered little or not at all from the great drought of 1276 to 1299. Perhaps the town was strong enough to protect itself from Shoshone raiders as it grew in size and strength with the addition of the less fortunate, the refugees that poured in from the north.

The town was in ruins, however, when a Jesuit priest named Father Eusebio Kino passed by in 1694—probably the first European to visit the site. During the next two centuries, Casa Grande (named by Father Kino) lay

No guided tours are given, but park rangers give ethnobotanic lectures every 45 minutes. Those interested should inquire at the information desk. Trail-guide leaflets are available upon request and are keyed to numbered stakes in the ruins area.

A small exhibit center displays examples of Hohokam ceramics and artifacts, as well as modern Indian arts and crafts. Also on display are several objects of unknown purpose discovered in the ruins. Offer your own suggestions about their use.

almost undisturbed. Then, in 1891, archaeologists from the Smithsonian Institution conducted initial excavations. Official monument status was bestowed in 1918.

Casa Grande is noteworthy for the unique construction techniques there; neither form nor brick was used. Instead, Hohokam builders simply piled up a two-foot–high layer of caliche mud, patted it into shape, let it dry, then added another layer, continuing to a height of four stories! A final finish of sieved caliche and water was then patted on as plaster.

The ground floor of Casa Grande itself was never used. For reasons as yet undiscovered, the bottom story was filled with earth to a level of five feet; short ladders were then used to reach the small entrance doorways. Casa Grande was undoubtedly the most elaborate structure in town, but it was never inhabited permanently. Its purpose is a mystery. Some archaeologists think it served a strictly religious function, much like the pyramids of Mexico; others believe the upper stories were used for astrological observations.

20 MILES

US 89

**7 WUPATKI NATIONAL
MONUMENT**

Sunset Crater

I 40

FLAGSTAFF

5

**WALNUT CANYON
NATIONAL MONUMENT**

I 40

US 89A   I 17

6

**TUZIGOOT NATIONAL
MONUMENT**

Sedona

Clarksdale

179

Cottonwood   279   US 89A

Exploring from
Flagstaff, Arizona

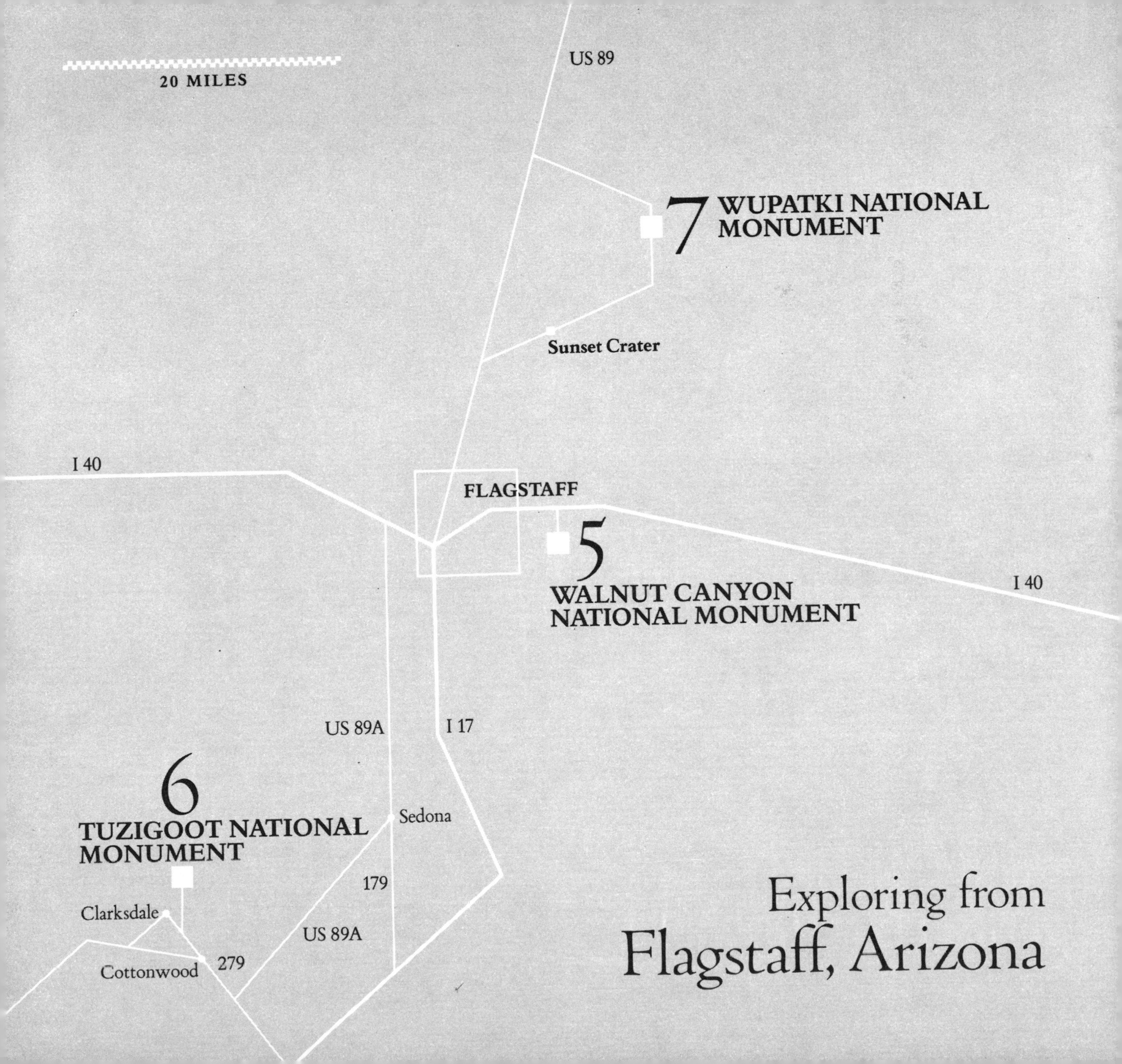

5 Walnut Canyon National Monument

S I N A G U A

HOURS   Summer, 7 A.M – 7 P.M.
daily. Winter, 8 A.M. – 5 P.M. daily.

ELEVATION   6690 feet.

ACRES   2249.

LOCATION   Seven and a half miles
east of Flagstaff, just off Interstate
40. A three-mile well-marked
entrance road connects monument
headquarters with the interstate.

ACCESS   A trip into Walnut
Canyon requires a .75-mile walk
and a vertical climb of 185 feet.
Going down isn't bad; coming out—
especially in the summer heat—is
another story. Visitors with heart or
respiratory ailments should take
frequent rests on trailside benches.
Sturdy shoes are a must, and in
summer carry a canteen.

FACILITIES   Drinking water, restrooms, and picnic areas are available; books are for sale at headquarters. Camping is not allowed.

INTERPRETIVE SERVICES   No guided
hikes are offered. Trail-guide leaflets
are available at the Visitor's Center
and are keyed to markers along the
trail. A small exhibit center contains
displays, and offers an introductory
slide program.

SITUATED in the mountainous terrain of the Coconino National Forest, Walnut Canyon is a narrow, sinuous, four-hundred-foot–deep
gash—its rim and sides heavily forested with juniper, pine, aspen, fir,
and cactus. The canyon takes its name from the Arizona black walnut
tree that grows wild in the area. About 400 small rooms in 120 individual cliff
dwellings are scattered along the length of the canyon. Most of the buildings
were constructed beneath horizontal limestone overhangs just beneath the
canyon rim. Only a few of the rooms have been restored.

Small groups of Sinagua migrated to Walnut Canyon about A.D. 1125,
when overpopulation and burned-out farmlands drove them from their traditional homes near the San Francisco Peaks. (See also *Montezuma Castle.*)

Dependent upon rainfall for moisture at Walnut Canyon, the Sinagua
grew crops of corn and beans in small, canyon-rim plots, heavily supplementing their diet as they could. Their pot had no preference; everything that could
be eaten, was—deer, mice, rats, birds, insects, roots, wild berries, and nuts.
Then in the early thirteenth century, rainfall in the area began to decrease; this
combined with infertility of the soil after a century's use caused crops to fail.
By 1275 the Walnut Canyon Sinagua had left, probably in a series of small
migrations. Archaeologists think they joined other clans of Sinagua in the
Verde Valley to the south.

So hidden and isolated were the Walnut Canyon ruins that they lay
almost undisturbed until the 1880s. Once discovered, however, many of the
dwellings were nearly destroyed by pot hunters and careless visitors. To protect the site from total obliteration, official monument status was bestowed
in 1915.

The astounding variety of geologic formations found in Walnut Canyon are visual treats. Worn by wind, eroded by water, and twisted by volcanic
upheaval, the canyon is dramatic evidence of the tremendous forces of nature.
Life in this rugged terrain must have been difficult indeed for the Sinagua
people.

6 Tuzigoot National Monument

HOURS 8 A.M. – 5 P.M. daily.

ELEVATION 3420 feet.

ACRES 57.

LOCATION Central Arizona, 51 miles southwest of Flagstaff. Take U.S. 89A south to Sedona, then west to Cottonwood. The monument entrance is 1.5 miles north of the Cottonwood town limits.

ACCESS A self-guiding, .25-mile trail winds through the ruins, ending at an overlook of the Verde River and nearby Black Hills. The trail is not strenuous.

FACILITIES Drinking water and restrooms are available at monument headquarters. Neither camping nor picnicking is allowed.

INTERPRETIVE SERVICES Advance reservations are required for guided hikes, offered only for large groups. No trail-guide leaflets available, but the paved trail is well marked with informative signs. The large exhibit center at Tuzigoot is probably the best in Arizona. Fine ceramics, jewelry, ornaments, and cloth are on display.

TUZIGOOT is a stabilized, partially restored, pueblo-style village, built atop a 125-foot–high hill overlooking the Verde River in the rolling hill country of the Upper Verde River Valley. Limestone blocks and river stones laid together with mud mortar were used for the village walls. At its peak, Tuzigoot contained more than 90 rooms.

Tuzigoot Pueblo and, to the south, Montezuma Castle underwent similar development. Groups of Sinagua moved south to the Verde Valley around A.D. 1125. From the valley's Hohokam inhabitants, they learned the practices of irrigation and above-ground house construction. Then, during the thirteenth century when drought conditions were becoming severe in the north, large numbers of Sinagua fled into the relatively lush Verde Valley. Tuzigoot, Montezuma Castle, and other nearby Indian towns tripled their populations as these new arrivals clustered along the Verde River and nearby spring-fed streams. Tensions increased over the next century; competition for arable land probably produced friction and even minor warfare among the clans of the Sinagua. By 1400, Tuzigoot had been abandoned. Archaeologists think the people may have joined Hohokam or Hopi villages in less populated areas.

Spanish explorer Antonio Espejo was probably the first European to visit Tuzigoot when he passed through the area in 1583. Afterward, the ruin lay undisturbed until, in 1933 and 1934, it was excavated by archaeologists from the University of Arizona. It gained official monument status in 1939 when the land it is on was donated to the federal government by the Phelps Dodge Corporation.

The noteworthy features at Tuzigoot include the unusual entryways. Probably for defensive purposes, few exterior doorways were built at Tuzigoot. Village inhabitants entered their dwellings by means of hatchlike openings in the roof, reached by wooden ladders from the ground floor.

7

Wupatki National Monument

S I N A G U A / A N A S A Z I

HOURS   Summer, 8 A.M. – 7 P.M. daily. Winter, 8 A.M. – 5 P.M. daily.

ELEVATION   4860–7000 feet.

ACRES   35,253.

LOCATION   North-central Arizona, 26 miles north of Flagstaff on U.S. 89. The monument entrance road is a loop, intersecting U.S. 89 in two places. The first intersection is marked "Sunset Crater"; the second (10 miles north) is marked "Wupatki National Monument." To cut 5 miles off your trip, take the second; the Visitor's Center is 14 miles east of the highway.

Wupatki Ruin, with San Francisco Peaks in the background.

WUPATKI National Monument consists of 56 square miles of volcanic wasteland—plain and mountain blanketed with a layer of fine volcanic ash and dotted with scrub conifer, cactus, and wild grasses. Within the boundaries of the monument are about eight hundred individual Indian dwellings. The four largest are accessible by road.

Four miles from the junction of U.S. 89 and the north monument entrance road is Lomaki Ruin, a small, mesa-top pueblo built of Moenkope sandstone. For the most part, the ruin is unexcavated. A short, unpaved side road gives access.

One-half mile east (along the main entrance road) is the Nalakihu-Citadel complex—a small, compact pueblo of 12 to 15 rooms, thought to house about 30 people at peak occupation, and also a larger, fortified, mesa-top pueblo of 30 to 35 rooms, thought to house about 60 people.

The largest ruin in the monument is Wupatki, a three-storied pueblo of a hundred rooms situated near the Visitor's Center. Thought to contain about three hundred people at peak occupation, Wupatki was probably the "hub" city of the Sinagua and Anasazi communities in the vicinity.

Three and a half miles south of Wupatki is Wukoki Ruin, an unusual, seven-room structure perched like a guardian upon the summit of a sandstone outcrop. Access to Wukoki is by a rough, unpaved side road. *This road is impassable in wet weather.*

From A.D. 600 until 1065, dry-farming communities of Sinagua lived quietly in the region near the San Francisco Peaks. They were a peaceful, friendly people, trading with both Anasazi communities to the north and Hohokam villages to the south. But in 1065 the situation changed dramatically when a nearby volcano (now Sunset Crater National Monument) erupted violently, covering more than eight hundred square miles with layers of hot cinders and fine ash. Frightened and alarmed, most of the area's occupants fled for their lives.

ACCESS Short, nonstrenuous trails lead to the four major ruins from their respective parking lots. Each is less than .5 mile in length.

BACKCOUNTRY A limited backpacking program to wilderness ruins is now offered at Wupatki, but special permission from the monument superintendent is required. Trails are not maintained in the region, so all hiking is cross-country.

During April and October, special guided backpack trips are offered to Crack in the Rock Ruin, a 14-mile round trip. Advance reservations are necessary.

FACILITIES Drinking water and restrooms, are available and books are for sale at Wupatki Ruin Visitor's Center. The monument has a single large picnic area, just off the north entrance road about 10 miles from the U.S. 89 junction. Camping is not allowed.

INTERPRETIVE SERVICES Guided hikes are offered for only the Wupatki Ruin trail, upon request. Trail-guide leaflets are available for the Wupatki, Nalakihu, and Citadel trails; they are keyed to numbered stakes at points of interest. Visitors are on their own at Lomaki and Wukoki. A small exhibit center at monument headquarters displays Sinagua pottery and artifacts.

As the Sinagua were later to discover, the explosion did more good than harm. The ash layer spewed out by the eruption added trace elements to the soil and trapped moisture from spring and autumn rains, consequently transforming the region into rich farmland. A few years after the eruption, the Sinagua returned—but not alone. As word of the potentially productive earth spread, Hohokam and Anasazi came too. By 1100, the San Francisco Peaks area had undergone a population boom and an estimated eight thousand people were living in the volcano's littered domain.

During the next quarter century, competition for arable land was fierce; in fact, many fields were used so heavily that they became infertile. Clans of Sinagua began moving south, to Walnut Canyon and into the Verde Valley. Those who remained, influenced by the building styles of the Anasazi stone masons (and perhaps with their assistance), erected the pueblos of Wupatki, Lomaki, the Citadel, and others. But by 1200, rainfall had decreased substantially, and overworked farmland was giving out. Perhaps minor warfare erupted among the clans, or at least unrest and anxiety. Unable to live in such harsh conditions, whether by mutual agreement or otherwise, farmers of all three cultures began migrating to more productive regions, and by 1225 the entire San Francisco Peaks area was deserted.

For the next eight hundred years, only passing settlers and an occasional sheepherder visited the dwellings beneath the great white peaks. Official monument status was bestowed in 1924. Major excavations took place in 1933, 1941, and 1952.

Two particularly noteworthy structures are found at Wupatki ruin—an amphitheaterlike depression complete with what seems to be a circle of seats, and a masonry ball court. The amphitheater was perhaps used for seasonal dances; the ball court, one of several discovered in Arizona, was probably after the Mexican style and used for *poc-ta-poc,* a game loosely resembling basketball.

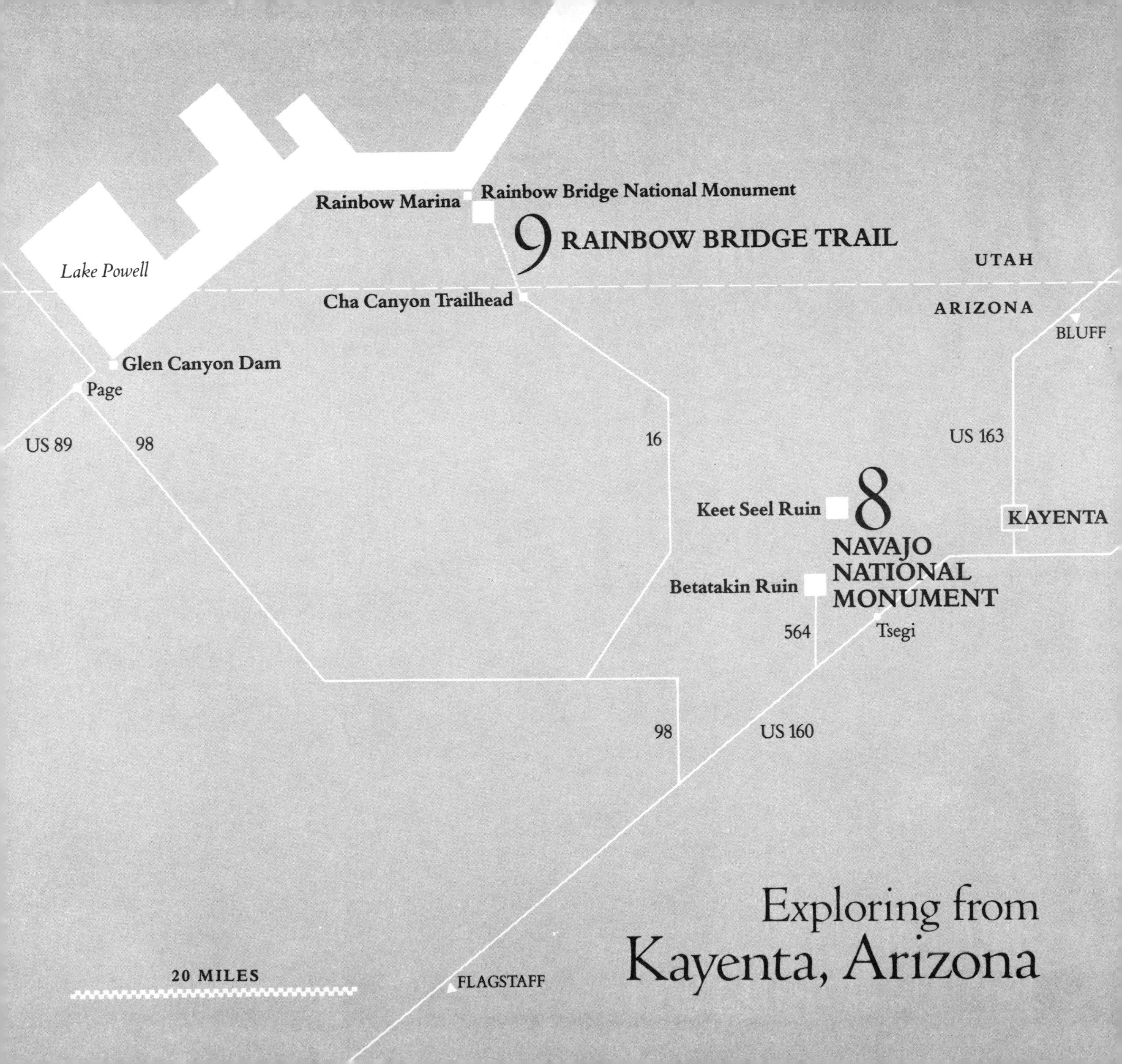

Rainbow Marina

Rainbow Bridge National Monument

9 RAINBOW BRIDGE TRAIL

UTAH

Lake Powell

Cha Canyon Trailhead

ARIZONA

BLUFF

Glen Canyon Dam

Page

US 89   98

16

US 163

Keet Seel Ruin **8**

KAYENTA

NAVAJO NATIONAL MONUMENT

Betatakin Ruin

564   Tsegi

98   US 160

Exploring from
Kayenta, Arizona

20 MILES

FLAGSTAFF

8   Navajo National Monument

A N A S A Z I

HOURS   Summer, 8 A.M. – 6 P.M. daily. Winter, 8 A.M. – 5 P.M. daily. Guided hikes, campfire programs, ruins access, campgrounds, and restrooms are open only as weather permits—usually from mid-May through mid-October.

ELEVATION   7286 feet.

ACRES   600.

LOCATION   Nineteen miles west of Kayenta on U.S. 160. A paved, nine-mile entrance road (Arizona 564) connects the main highway with monument headquarters.

ACCESS   To visit Keet Seel requires a reservation for a backcountry trip. Betatakin can be visited without a reservation, but only in the company of a park ranger. The round trip to Betatakin, over a steep, extremely rugged trail (with a seven hundred vertical feet rise), requires three hours. Visitors should wear sturdy shoes and carry drinking water. Four hikes per day are led; the 20 people on each hike join the group on a first-come, first-served basis. Trips leave every two

Betatakin Ruin.

SITUATED in the rugged, sandstone canyon country of northeast Arizona, Navajo National Monument is one of the most beautiful Park Service domains in the western states. Only two ruins can be visited in this monument, but both are spectacular. Betatakin Ruin, nearest to monument headquarters, is a 135-room cliff palace, on the floor and upper back wall of a five-hundred-foot–high natural amphitheater in boxlike Betatakin Canyon. The ruins have been completely excavated. Below them on the canyon floor, bounding away in disheveled loveliness, is a deep forest of aspen, Douglas fir, and oak. Keet Seel Ruin, eight miles into the backcountry, is a 160-room village, also situated in a natural sandstone alcove. It is the largest cliff ruin in Arizona and probably the best preserved prehistoric Indian ruin in the United States. It too has been completely excavated.

The great redrock canyons of Betatakin, Keet Seel, and Nitsin (the latter containing Inscription House Ruin, now closed to the public indefinitely) were sparsely occupied by pithouse and cave-dwelling seminomads about the time of Christ. These early people, who sustained themselves by a combination of hunting, gathering, and primitive agriculture, are now called Basketmaker Anasazi. (Basketmakers used primitive pottery but are known mainly for their fine woven baskets.)

About A.D. 600, Basketmaker lifestyles underwent a change. Farming became the primary source of food. Using primitive "digging sticks," farmers cultivated corn, squash, and beans in canyon-bottom plots, irrigating their crops with flood runoff or depending totally upon rainfall. Turkeys and dogs had been domesticated, and a better type of pottery was in use. Above-ground villages had replaced the brush-covered, subterranean pithouses and canyonside caves.

Basketmaker artifacts found in the amphitheaters of both Betatakin and Keet Seel suggest that there the Anasazi took temporary shelter under overhangs in early times, but construction did not begin on either town until about 1250. The first dwellings were small, and the site was occupied by only hours, beginning at 8 A.M. Those not interested in visiting the actual ruins may view the site from an overlook reached by a one-mile–round-trip trail that begins at the Visitor's Center.

BACKCOUNTRY   Backcountry travel is allowed only to Keet Seel, which is open from mid-May through only mid-September. The 16-mile–round-trip horseback ride along the steep, primitive trail to Keet Seel must be taken under the supervision of a Navajo guide. The full-day trip requires a reservation, which will be accepted no less than a day before the ride but no more than two months in advance. Wear a hat and long pants, and carry your own water and sack lunch.

Overnight hikes are allowed only to Keet Seel. Reservations are necessary, and hikers must sign in and obtain a trail-guide leaflet and backcountry permit at monument headquarters. The hike—across part of the Navajo Reservation—is rugged, without potable water, and requires two full days for the 16-mile round trip.

Betatakin Ruin from the canyon floor.

All travel in Navajo National Monument is by leave of the Navajo Indians. When hiking, move quietly, build no fires, carry out everything you carry in, and disturb neither artifact nor the environment. Don't attempt to sneak onto the Betatakin trail without a ranger along. (Many people do.) A locked gate halfway down the steep trail is impassable without a key.

Note also that local streams are polluted; don't take a drink. Be wary of poison ivy and biting red ants in the bottom of Betatakin Canyon.

FACILITIES Drinking water, restrooms, books for sale, and a gift shop are found at monument headquarters. The monument has a small picnic area and a 30-site campground with tables, water, and fireplaces. Wood is not to be gathered here, so bring your own charcoal. Reservations are not needed except for backcountry use, but no RVs longer than 25 feet are permitted.

INTERPRETIVE SERVICES Trail-guide leaflets are available only for the Keet Seel trail, but the Betatakin rangers are talkative and full of information. A small museum displays Anasazi artifacts and offers a slide show and a reconstructed Indian village.

a few people. Twenty years later, almost as if new arrivals were expected, major building projects were underway. By 1290 both cliff cities were at peak population, Betatakin with about 125 inhabitants and Keet Seel with about 150. But within a few years construction ceased and population declined. By 1300, both towns were deserted.

Curiously, the occupation of both Keet Seel and Betatakin began and their populations increased almost in parallel with the onset and increased severity of drought conditions in the Southwest. This may indicate that Anasazi clans in other, drier parts of the region saw hardship coming and dispatched a few families to seek havens. Perhaps, as rainfall decreased at home, such scout families sent back word that water and arable land had been found. Why the isolated cities were abandoned after only two generations of occupation, however, remains a mystery.

Keet Seel was first discovered by amateur archaeologists Richard Wetherill and Charlie Mason in 1895. Fourteen years later Richard's brother John Wetherill, accompanied by professional archaeologist Byron Cummings, found Betatakin while on an exploration trip to another canyon. Strangely enough, Navajo National Monument was officially established in 1909 several months before Betatakin's discovery.

At Betatakin, the construction is worthy of special attention. The amphitheater floor is so steep that Anasazi masons had to "glue" building foundations to the sloping rock with huge amounts of mud. And because of the sloping floor, the inhabitants were unable to construct traditional underground *kivas* (religious or ceremonial rooms). Instead, above-ground ceremonial structures called *kihus* were erected, using thick, double-walled masonry to create the isolation and silence of an underground room.

For greater security on the site's precarious perch, Keet Seel masons constructed a massive retaining wall across parts of the amphitheater's entrance. One hundred and eighty feet in length, 11 feet high in some places, the wall's rear portion was filled with tons of earth. This leveled the amphitheater's floor and created a wide avenue upon which inhabitants could walk in safety.

Petroglyphs at Betatakin include a symbol of the Hopi Fire Clan. The presence of this symbol on a wall at the east end of the ruin has led Hopi elders to claim the site as an original Hopi settlement.

9   Rainbow Bridge Trail

A N A S A Z I

BEST HIKING TIMES   April, May, September, October.

TRAIL LENGTH   15–20 strenuous miles.

ELEVATION   3700–6300 feet.

LOCATION   50 miles northeast of Glen Canyon Dam.

ACCESS   The trail is reached by boat or car, as described in the text.

"Nonnezoshi"—"Rainbow Turned to Stone."

THE sandstone arch called Rainbow Bridge may have had ceremonial significance for the ancient Indians, but on the Rainbow Bridge Trail the route itself is the main attraction. This rugged wilderness trail meanders east from Rainbow Bridge National Monument—situated in a side canyon of Lake Powell in Utah—and ends in an isolated part of the Navajo Indian Reservation northwest of Kayenta, Arizona. Scattered along its length are literally hundreds of nameless, unexcavated Anasazi dwellings. Most have been consumed by centuries of wind and weather, yet the beauty of the surrounding landscape adds splendor to their decay. Traversing a dozen magnificent, red-ochre slickrock canyons, the trail circumnavigates the northern slopes of 10,284-foot Navajo Mountain, then drops into Surprise Valley, a lovely and surprisingly lush slickrock basin made famous in Zane Grey's *Riders of the Purple Sage.*

Hikers can reach the trailheads by two ways only. The quickest is by boat—from Glen Canyon Dam on Lake Powell to Rainbow Bridge National Monument, 50 miles up-lake. Shuttle boats carry passengers from Wahweap Marina (near the dam) to the monument several times a day for a reasonable cost. Rental boats are also available at Wahweap. The trailhead begins at the base of Rainbow Bridge itself; it is unmarked but is the only trail leading east from the bridge.

The eastern trailhead can be reached by road from Kayenta. Take U.S. 160 west to the Arizona 98 junction, and turn right toward Page. Turn right again 14 miles north onto Navajo 16, a rough dirt road leading to Navajo Mountain. (*Occasionally this road is washed out by flash floods; check conditions in Kayenta before taking Navajo 16.*) Stay on this road for 35 miles, then, at a Y, take the right-hand junction to Navajo Mountain Trading Post, about 6 miles. Three and seven-tenths miles past the Trading Post, go straight through a four-way intersection. At a second Y, 2.8 miles farther, take the left-hand fork. This road will cross an earthen dam and shortly thereafter fork again. Take the left fork. The road ends at the Cha Canyon trailhead, about 1.5 miles farther on.

CAUTION The entire length of the Rainbow Bridge Trail is extremely rugged; some portions, because of unprotected exposure to steep drop-offs, are dangerous. Rock-falls, lightning storms, and flash floods are not uncommon, especially in July and August. Rattlesnakes and scorpions are seldom seen but ever present. Hikers should be in good physical shape.

Almost every canyon has a permanent stream, even during midsummer, but most are polluted by livestock. Carry your own water—at least a gallon per day per person. No facilities exist, here, and no interpretive services.

If you meet Navajos on the trail, be courteous. Show your permit and tell them where you are going. Leave all gates as you find them, and stay clear of hogans (Navajo houses) and livestock.

A corn storage bin in Surprise Valley.

A permit is needed to hike on the Navajo Reservation. Permits are available from Navajo Tribal Headquarters in Window Rock, Arizona. You will also need a route map. Accurate maps, however, are few and far between. A hand-drawn, mimeographed map and hiker's instructions can be obtained from the National Park Service headquarters at the Glen Canyon National Recreation Area in Page, Arizona. Topographical maps can be obtained from any southwest office of the U.S. Geological Survey. Ask for the map of the Navajo Mountain Section, 15 Minute Quadrangle, Arizona/Utah. *Do not attempt this trail without good maps.* Guided horseback trips are sometimes available; inquire at the Navajo Mountain Trading Post.

The exact origin of the Rainbow Bridge Trail has been lost in time, but probably the pathway was constructed originally to give local groups of Anasazi access to the Colorado River, to their west. Rainbow Bridge, too, may have played some role in the trail's construction; the great natural arch may have had some religious significance in the local Anasazi culture.

After the general Anasazi exodus from the Four Corners region about A.D. 1300, the trail lay unused for perhaps five centuries before Paiute and Navajo Indians once again followed it to "Nonnezoshi"—the "Rainbow Turned to Stone." The first white men to tread the ancient pathway were probably prospectors searching the slickrock for gold during the late 1800s. The trail's recorded history dates from 1909, when Byron Cummings, W. B. Douglass, and John Wetherill first entered the isolated region in search of the legendary Rainbow Bridge.

Many of the larger Anasazi ruins along the trail, especially those in Surprise Valley, are marked with the initials JW, for John Wetherill. An amateur archaeologist, Wetherill was probably the first white visitor to most of the ruins. He left his initials not purposely to deface the ruins but simply as a reminder to himself that he had been to those sites, in case he returned.

Once the trail was rediscovered, it was used by such noteworthy explorers as Zane Grey and Teddy Roosevelt, who came to view Rainbow Bridge. In 1933, portions of the original Anasazi path were bypassed when new, more easily negotiated sections were blasted out of solid rock by the Civilian Conservation Corps so that Navajo Indians could bring their sheep to water. In the early 1960s, Glen Canyon Dam was completed, which filled Lake Powell, giving easy access to Rainbow Bridge by boat. The trail was almost forgotten. Even today, it is seldom used except by Navajos.

The rugged, sandstone canyon country surrounding Bluff, Utah, was a major center of Anasazi activity between A.D. 800 and 1300. No one knows exactly how many dwellings exist in the vicinity of Bluff, but certainly there are thousands. Almost every cliff or canyon slope within a 50-mile radius of the town presents some sign of ancient occupation, whether a simple pottery shard or a 30-room village.

Visitors to the Bluff area should realize, however, that this is one of the most remote regions in the United States, and off-road travel without a guide is foolhardy and dangerous. Name any backcountry hazard— rattlesnakes to rockfalls to flash floods—and the slickrock offers it. Be well advised never to leave maintained roads unless you are acquainted with the country or accompanied by someone who is.

To describe more than a few major sites in the space allowed by this book would be impossible. Those who wish to explore the slickrock more thoroughly can arrange for a guided tour, by foot or four-wheel-drive vehicle, through local outfitters. Two extremely knowledgeable guide agencies operate in the Bluff area—Gene Foushee and his Recapture Lodge Tours in Bluff itself, and Goulding's Trading Post near Monument Valley Navajo Park. Either can provide the information you desire or full-fledged backcountry tours.

Exploring from
Bluff, Utah

Monticello

US 163

US 666

95

12 NATURAL BRIDGES
NATIONAL MONUMENT

Blanding

Pleasant
View

263

95

11
HOVENWEEP
NATIONAL
MONUMENT

261

13

GRAND GULCH
PRIMITIVE AREA

BLUFF

262

14 COMB WASH

Aneth

Mexican Hat

20 MILES

US 163

UTAH   COLORADO

Gouldings

10 MONUMENT VALLEY NAVAJO
TRIBAL PARK

ARIZONA   NEW MEXICO

US 160

504

Monument Valley Navajo Tribal Park

A N A S A Z I

HOURS 8 A.M. – 5 P.M. daily. Hours are subject to change without notice.

ELEVATION 5400 feet.

AREA 1600 square miles.

LOCATION The park headquarters straddles the Utah-Arizona border, 47 miles southwest of Bluff on U.S. 163.

ACCESS A 16-mile unpaved loop beginning at tribal park headquarters winds through Monument Valley. It can be negotiated in a passenger car in good weather. Only a few of the ruins can be reached from this road, however. A guide is necessary on this terrain, and in any case unaccompanied backcountry exploring is strictly forbidden by the Navajos. Full-day commercial tours are offered by Recapture Lodge in Bluff, and by Goulding's Trading Post near park headquarters.

Monument Valley.

REFERRED to as the "Eighth Wonder of the World," Monument Valley has one of the most beautiful desert landscapes on earth. It is a land of towering buttes and juniper-studded mesas, of sandstone pinnacles and tortured hobgoblins of stone, all of varied and ever-changing hue. Scattered through this wonderland of stone and sand, especially in the southwest portion of the park (the Mystery Valley section), are several hundred Anasazi dwellings—most of them small, all of them unnamed and unmarked. The majority are cliff houses, tucked away in isolated canyons and hidden amphitheaters well out of sight of the nearest roads. Only with a well-informed guide can most of the ruins be reached.

Little is known about the Monument Valley Anasazi except that they were firmly ensconced in this sandstone wilderness by A.D. 900, farming small plots of desert earth, depending upon rain and flood runoff for moisture, supplementing their meager diet with small game and wild plants.

Water was a problem—always. Indeed, some evidence suggests that the valley's inhabitants constructed small dams to trap and hold flash-flood runoff as it flowed down the arroyos after each rain. Crops were probably planted on the arroyo edges, thereby being watered when the dams caused overflows. Because of the water situation, the Anasazi here were probably ignored by enemies. Even a mild drought would have been disastrous, however; and as rainfall began to decrease in the Southwest about the middle of the twelfth century, most of the Monument Valley Anasazi abandoned their homes to join other clans whose access to water was less limited.

Today, pottery and projectile points still blanket the ground in places. The present-day Indians, the Navajo, would prefer to keep it that way. Several hundred Navajo families reside in this arid desert, their lives almost unchanged in two centuries. Though unrelated to the original Anasazi inhabitants, the Navajos exist in a fashion similar to that of the agriculturalists gone now for eight hundred years. Isolated and clannish, dependent upon the land and little else for survival, they are, in a sense, a living reminder of the past.

A small Anasazi cliff dwelling in Mystery Valley (left). Monument Valley.

CAUTION   Keep no artifacts; do not, in fact, attempt to enter or even locate any ruin without a guide. Always be aware that you are in rugged, isolated country where help is far away. Many sections of road in Monument Valley are vulnerable to flash floods in rainy weather; others are so sandy, travel even in a four-wheel-drive vehicle is not recommended. When driving your own car, always carry drinking water, food, and extra automobile parts.

FACILITIES   Drinking water, restrooms, books for sale, and a gift shop can be found at park headquarters; gasoline, food, and lodging are available at nearby Goulding's Trading Post or in Bluff. Inside the park, a 15-site modern campground is situated adjacent to the Visitor's Center; nearby is a primitive campground with pit toilets. A large and well-equipped KOA private campground is near Goulding's. No facilities exist in the backcountry, and no interpretive services are offered.

Hovenweep National Monument

A N A S A Z I

Hovenweep Castle.

NUMEROUS single dwellings and small Anasazi villages lie hidden in the rolling canyon country east of Bluff, many of them unnamed and unmarked even on the most detailed maps. The largest ruin under National Park Service protection is the Square Tower Group—13 major dwellings, most of them now fully excavated, constructed in or along the edge of Ruin Canyon.

Perhaps the most eye-catching structure in this ancient community is Hovenweep Castle, a D-shaped, two-story building perched in a fortresslike position at the head of Ruin Canyon. It is constructed so close to the canyon's lip that even lizards are nervous clinging to the outer Castle wall. Directly below is the monument's most unusual building, Square Tower, a 20-foot-high stone spire of uncertain function built on the narrow canyon floor. The remaining dwellings of the Square Tower Group extend eastward for about a mile along the canyon's edge.

Within a 10-mile radius of the Square Tower Group lie five other major sites—Holly Ruin, Hackberry Ruin, Cutthroat Castle, Horseshoe Ruin, and Cajon Ruin—all reachable by road. Most of these outliers, like the dwellings at Square Tower, were built at canyon's edge, and mostly near its head. All are constructed with stone blocks mortared with mud, and some are unique in their architecture. One building at Holly Ruin, for instance, is round on the outside but square inside; another, this one at Horseshoe Ruin, consists of two concentric circles of unconnected rooms. Needless to say, the functions of both structures are mysteries.

What is known is that by A.D. 900 the Hovenweep region was inhabited and dominated by Anasazi farmers. Originally they came from the crowded pueblos at Mesa Verde, nearly a hundred miles to the east. Perhaps they were migrants, perhaps outcasts. Whatever they were, by the tenth century these Anasazi were living at Hovenweep in small, scattered villages and making the land bloom with plots of corn, beans, squash, and melons.

By 1200, annual rainfall had decreased substantially. The outlying farm villages were abandoned and new ones constructed near canyons containing permanent springs. The style and location of these new structures suggest that the Anasazi were also preparing for attack.

Whether the attackers were Shoshone raiders or perhaps other clans of Anasazi who coveted Hovenweep water resources is unknown. But even a

Anasazi hand prints on a cave wall in the backcountry of Hovenweep.

strong defense did little to protect these people from the devastating drought of the thirteenth century. As even permanent springs disappeared, the Hovenweep Anasazi were forced once again to leave their homes. Archaeologists think some may have joined Zuni Pueblo in western New Mexico. By 1300, the entire region was deserted.

A Mormon expedition, passing through the country in 1854, was probably the first group of non-Indians to see the ruins at Hovenweep. The site's name, a Ute word meaning "Deserted Valley," was bestowed by frontier photographer William Jackson, who visited in 1874. Official monument status was given in 1923.

In recent times, many theories (each associated with an archaeologist) have been put forward to explain the purpose of the Hovenweep towers, such as the one at the Square Tower Group. The majority of these structures were probably meant to be defensive, since they are situated near water sources, each has only a single tiny doorway, and many of these entryways are protected by parapets. In addition, most of the towers have peepholes pointing outwards—away from the canyon.

Some structures, however, served another purpose. At least three sites in the monument (including Square Tower) were primitive observatories. Certain of their windows are situated so that during the summer and winter solstices (about June 22 and December 22) and the autumn and vernal equinoxes (about September 23 and March 21) sunlight entering the openings would strike particular points of interior wall. At no other time of year would light reach those points.

Why did the Anasazi mark these dates? The reason is a combination of agriculture and ceremony. The vernal equinox marks the beginning of planting season; the autumn equinox marks the time of harvest. During the winter solstice the sun reaches its southernmost point in the sky; knowing this, the Anasazi could begin proper ceremonies to assure its return northward, bringing with it greater warmth and the beginning of the growing season. The summer solstice is the longest day of the year; ceremonies then perhaps assured that cool nights would not disappear altogether.

12

Natural Bridges National Monument, White Canyon

A N A S A Z I

HOURS 8 A.M. – 4:30 P.M. daily.

ELEVATION 6500 feet.

ACRES 7600.

LOCATION Fifty-two miles northwest of Bluff. Take U.S. 163 about 20 miles north to the junction of Utah 95. Turn left and follow 95 to the monument entrance road 32 miles farther, on the right. The alternate route is to take U.S. 163 south about 24 miles to the Utah 261 junction. Follow 261 north about 33 miles to Utah 95, and turn left to the monument entrance road.

White Canyon.

MOST of the Anasazi dwellings in Natural Bridges National Monument—about two hundred sites—lie within the narrow confines of White Canyon, a serpentlike chasm running northeast to southwest through the monument's entire length. Few of the ruins have been excavated and, with the exception of Bare Ladder Ruin and Horse Collar Ruin (visible from overlooks), any access to them requires strenuous hikes into White Canyon.

Because so little archaeological study has been done in Natural Bridges, occupation dates for White Canyon's numerous ruins are unknown. Since Anasazi communities in adjacent areas were flourishing by A.D. 800, however, the cliff dwellers of White Canyon probably were, too.

The population here was not large, probably not more than several hundred. Even so, sustenance must have been scanty at best. Anasazi farmers grew crops of corn and beans in small plots along the canyon's bottom, but owing to limited space, harvests must have been small. Most of the ruins contain a great number of kivas, suggesting perhaps that constant spiritual ceremony was necessary to ensure survival, especially when food supplies were in short supply.

When did these particular Anasazi abandon their homes? Did they too suffer predation from Shoshone nomads or wandering clans of other Anasazi, even in this isolated, almost inaccessible canyon? Both questions are unanswered. Near several of the ruins, however, Hopi clan symbols can be seen, indicating that White Canyon Anasazi may have joined the homogenous club of present-day–Hopi ancestors.

Natural Bridges and many White Canyon ruins were first visited by prospectors in the 1880s. Official monument status was bestowed in 1908.

Natural Bridges derives its name from three massive stone arches that were created as rampant streams, wind, and ice gradually carved channels through the bases of sandstone fins. These natural wonders should not be

ACCESS   Many of the ruins in Natural Bridges are restricted by the National Park Service because of their fragile nature and previous destruction by artifact hunters. Two of the largest, however, can be viewed from overlooks along Bridge View Drive, and a number of others may be explored by visitors who don't mind walking. To see Bare Ladder Ruin, park in the first, right-hand pullout past the campground entrance, then walk to White Canyon's lip (200 yards to the right). To view Horse Collar Ruin, park in the third pullout past the Bridge Canyon Drive picnic area and walk to the rim (.25 mile to the right). Neither pullout is marked. Monument officials request that people who wish to visit other ruins in White Canyon obtain permission and trail maps from the Visitor's Center at monument headquarters.

BACKCOUNTRY   Overnight back-country hiking is prohibited, but day hikes are encouraged. Trail guides are available at most trail-heads and the Visitor's Center. Hikers should stop at monument headquarters to check in and obtain information about the White Canyon ruins. All trails in the monument are steep and strenuous, so carry plenty of drinking water and wear sturdy shoes.

FACILITIES   Drinking water and restrooms are available and books and film for sale at monument headquarters. A 13-site campground and a small picnic area are east of headquarters along Bridge View Drive. Reservations are not required.

INTERPRETIVE SERVICES   A small geologic museum and an introductory slide program detail the history and prehistory of the monument but give little information concerning the Anasazi occupants. Guided tours are given to large groups upon request, but are led only to the bridges. (The rangers here do not give out information about Natural Bridges Anasazi ruins unless asked. Some people might think this is being overprotective, but previous destruction by pot hunters has made monument officials wary. A single Anasazi pot in good condition will bring $5000 on the open market.)

ignored when you visit the monument. All can be viewed from overlooks along Bridge View Drive, the paved road circumnavigating the monument's 7600 acres.

Bare Ladder Ruin overlook with White Canyon below.

13

Grand Gulch Primitive Area

A N A S A Z I

BEST HIKING TIMES March, April, May, September, October.

ELEVATION 4400–6400 feet.

LOCATION About 45 miles northwest of Bluff. Take U.S. 163 south to the Utah 261 junction and turn right. Stay on 261 for about 29 miles to the Kane Gulch Ranger Station.

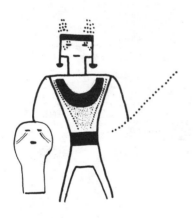

Corn storage bins in a Grand Gulch side canyon.

GRAND Gulch is similar to White Canyon in Natural Bridges National Monument; a winding, many-fingered, 50-mile–long canyon slicing northeast to southwest through the juniper-covered mesa country of southeastern Utah. Within the canyon complex are several hundred small Anasazi dwellings, most of them unexcavated cliff houses. In addition, thousands of petroglyphs and pictographs can be found along the canyon's walls.

Grand Gulch was occupied as early as A.D. 200 by Basketmaker Anasazi, but there are indications that the canyon was abandoned around 800. Why, no one knows. Two centuries later the region was reoccupied and remained so until the Anasazi exodus at the end of the thirteenth century.

The people here were farmers, but unlike their neighbors in White Canyon they preferred to farm the mesa tops instead of canyon floors. Along the Grand Gulch lip are hundreds of ancient agricultural plots, most of them adjacent to check dams and diversion canals built to trap and hold rainfall runoff. In addition to farming, the people utilized many wild foods, such as mule deer, bighorn sheep, rabbits, squirrels, rats, mice, rice grass, yucca, and cactus. They had domesticated turkeys as well; recent excavations of an Anasazi cave dwelling suggest that entire communities did little throughout their lives except to care for these big birds. Turkeys and people lived side by side in the caves—probably not a very sanitary existence.

The Anasazi's use of the turkey is somewhat mysterious. Some archaeologists say the Anasazi used the bird as a source only of feathers and not of food, a theory based on the absence of turkey bones in most Anasazi dwellings and refuse heaps. At the excavation in Grand Gulch, for example, only one turkey skeleton was found amidst thousands of feathers, remnants of turkey-feather blankets, and several centuries of turkey manure. Other archaeologists, however, find this theory difficult to swallow. Pre-Columbian life in the Southwest was severe; why then should Indians ignore a plentiful food source so near at hand? Offer your suggestions to your neighborhood archaeologist.

ACCESS   The ruins can be reached only by strenuous hiking. Several primitive roads lead from Highway 261 to within walking distance of the Primitive Area boundary (beyond which no cars are allowed). However, these roads were not made for passenger cars, and are not recommended for unguided travel, even in a four-wheel-drive vehicle.

Access into Grand Gulch is by foot and is easiest from the Kane Gulch Ranger Station (which offers no facilities or interpretive services). A trail follows the canyon to its junction with the San Juan River, 53 miles to the west. Hiking is strenuous, and any trip of more than a few miles requires an over-night stay in the canyon.

Since Grand Gulch is an official National Primitive Area, permits are required; they may be obtained, along with hiker's maps and instructions, at Kane Gulch. Group size is restricted to 25; horseback parties and groups of more than 15 are required to make advance reservations. Camping is prohibited within a hundred feet of any water source.

CAUTION   Here, as everywhere in the slickrock, a number of dangers await the careless hiker. Rattlesnakes, scorpions, rock falls, and flash floods are commonly encountered. In summer heat stroke, particularly, is a hazard; 115-degree temperatures are not unusual.

After the Anasazi left, in about 1300, Grand Gulch lay unvisited for centuries until, in the 1880s, ranch cowboys discovered many of the ruins. Some excavation took place in 1893–94 by archaeologists from the American Museum of Natural History. Today the canyon is protected by the Bureau of Land Management.

The rim of Grand Gulch.

14 Comb Wash

ANASAZI

ELEVATION   4700 feet.

LOCATION   Take U.S. 163 to the Comb Wash bridge, about 7 miles south of Bluff. There, an unpaved road suitable only for foot or four-wheel-drive travel turns off the highway onto the canyon floor.

ACCESS   Most dwellings and petroglyph sites in Comb Wash can be reached by the canyon-bottom road, but the sites are unmarked and the road can be negotiated by vehicles only with four-wheel drive. *The road should not be attempted in a passenger car.* Guided four-wheel-drive tours can be arranged at Recapture Lodge in Bluff.

BACKCOUNTRY   The wash is Bureau of Land Management land. It has no facilities or interpretive services, but also no restrictions on backpacking or hiking except to respect the environment and take nothing from the ruins. The Comb Wash road gives access to all points in the canyon. Topographical maps of the region can be obtained in any Southwest office of the U.S. Geological Survey.

Snake House Ruin.

ORTY miles in length but no more than a mile wide, Comb Wash begins in the Manti La Sal National Forest north of Blanding, Utah, and winds southward to end in confluence with the San Juan River a few miles west of Bluff. This great, stony ditch is the result of water slowly wearing a path through escarpments of Wingate and Navajo sandstone, laid down as dunes millions of years ago.

Scattered along the length of the wash are hundreds of Anasazi dwellings, most of them badly eroded by 10 centuries of desert wind. More interesting than the dwellings, however, are the thousands of petroglyphs that in some places blanket the canyon wall. Most are what we would call nonsensical symbols, perhaps understood by the original artist; perhaps not. Humanoid figures and desert animals are carved, as well.

Most of the Comb Wash ruins are small, suggesting the canyon was probably only a temporary home; and since the area has undergone little archaeological study, occupation dates are speculative. Because of its permanent source of water, the wash was perhaps occupied in desperation when drought conditions became severe elsewhere. Even here, though, the stream finally failed, and before 1300 the canyon was abandoned.

Cowboys, prospectors, and early settlers visited Comb Wash often in the late 1800s. One of the most interesting visits to Comb Wash was that in 1880 by a large group of Mormon settlers, under orders from Brigham Young to colonize the San Juan River area around present-day Bluff. For several months they had been on the trail—250 men, women, and children, almost 90 wagons, and several hundred head of livestock—and had had to literally blast a road across the slickrock. Near the Colorado River, the group had accomplished an almost unbelievable feat, lowering the entire wagon train down a near-vertical two-thousand–foot cliff to the river below, and losing only one mule in the process.

When they reached Comb Wash, one of the last obstacles standing between the settlers and their destination, they attempted the Colorado River trick in reverse, blasting a road up a sheer wall to gain access to the canyon rim. When the path was finished, the train crept up the sheer sandstone to the top only to find impassable cliffs on the other side. Another route, this one more successful, was chosen, and the long trip ended a few days later. The old Mormon wagon trail can still be seen and visited.

Petroglyphs in Comb Wash.

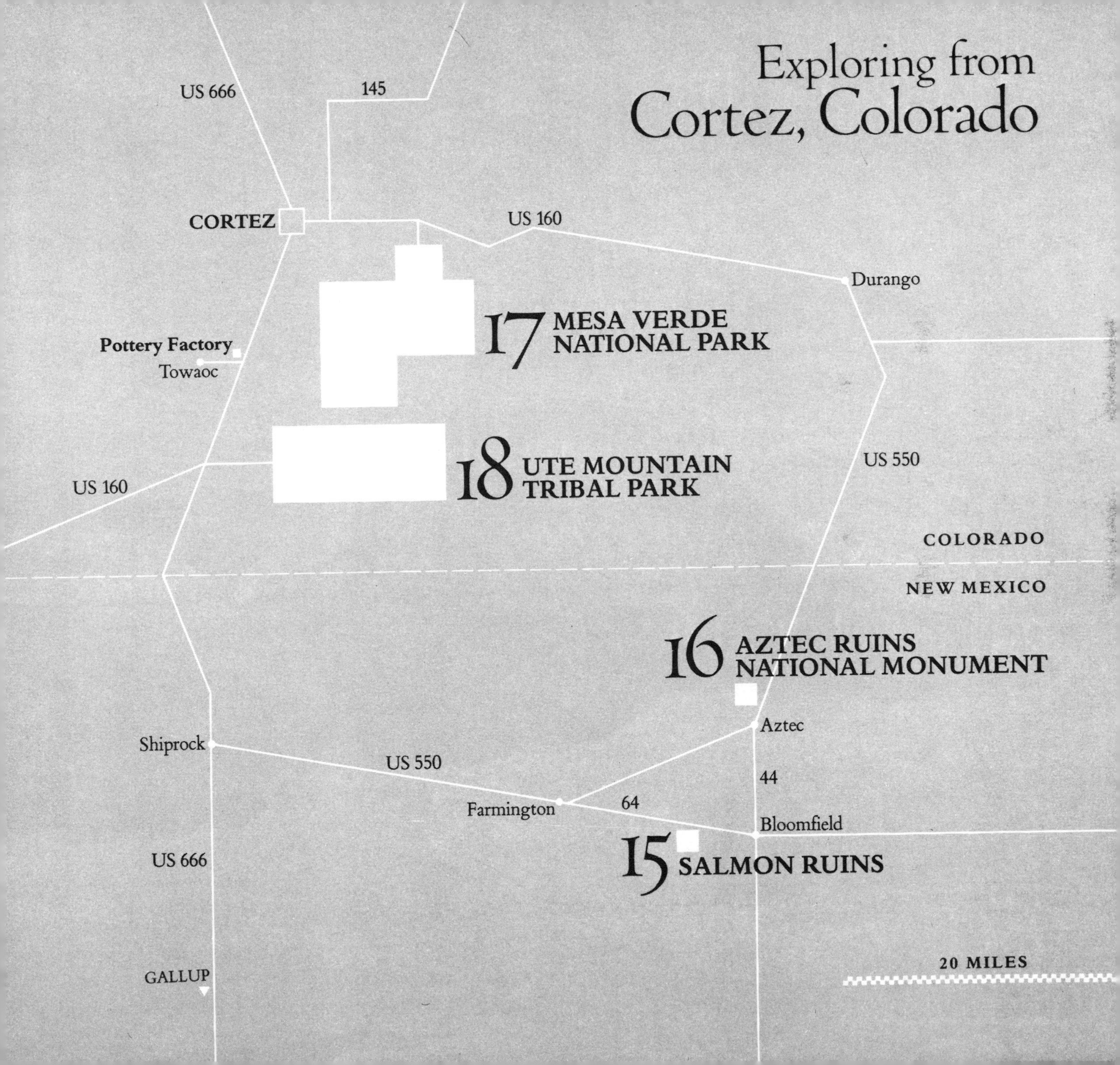

Exploring from
Cortez, Colorado

US 666   145

CORTEZ

US 160

Durango

17 MESA VERDE
NATIONAL PARK

Pottery Factory

Towaoc

18 UTE MOUNTAIN
TRIBAL PARK

US 550

US 160

COLORADO

NEW MEXICO

16 AZTEC RUINS
NATIONAL MONUMENT

Aztec

Shiprock

US 550

44

Farmington   64

Bloomfield

US 666

15 SALMON RUINS

GALLUP

20 MILES

Salmon Ruins
(San Juan County Research Center)

ANASAZI

A selection of prehistoric pottery excavated from Salmon Ruins.

THIS apartment-house–type dwelling (originally four stories) consists of 250 rooms built in the shape of a squared C, and it sits atop a low rise overlooking the verdant San Juan River Valley. Only a portion of the ruin has been excavated. In A.D. 1088, migrants from Chaco Canyon (50 miles to the south) began construction here on what archaeologists call a Chaco outlier—a small community built to alleviate overpopulation and to furnish agricultural products. Both the Salmon and Aztec pueblos (see *Aztec Ruins National Monument*) were connected to Chaco Canyon by a 40-foot–wide "highway." Since the Anasazi had no pack animals except dogs, all transport was by human endeavor. The highway was equipped with rest houses containing food, water, and sleeping quarters.

Salmon was completed by 1095. Unlike other Anasazi communities there was a stream from which a constant supply of water could be drawn. If, however, Salmon and other outliers were built in an effort to save a crumbling culture, the effort failed. About 1130, the pueblo was abandoned.

A century passed. About 1230, Salmon was reoccupied by people from Mesa Verde. In 1250, a great fire swept through the pueblo, and 50 children were killed when a roof collapsed. Salmon was abandoned for a short period while the buildings were repaired, then reoccupied. But 20 years later another fire destroyed almost the entire pueblo. The town was abandoned permanently.

The ruin site was homesteaded in the 1870s by George Salmon, whose family protected it from treasure seekers. In 1967, it was sold to the San Juan Museum Association, which with federal help funded the first excavations and constructed the Visitor's Center and exhibit area. Noteworthy today are the techniques and materials that the original Chaco masons used to construct Salmon. Instead of working with the substandard local rock, they quarried and shaped thousands of sandstone blocks 5 miles away, then carried them to the site by hand. Instead of cutting soft cottonwood trees near the pueblo for roof timbers, the Chacoans felled pine logs in the mountains 35 miles away, then floated them down the San Juan River to Salmon.

16 Aztec Ruins National Monument

ANASAZI

HOURS   Summer, 8 A.M. – 7 P.M. daily. Winter, 8 A.M. – 5 P.M. daily. Closed on Christmas and New Year's Day.

ELEVATION   5640.

ACRES   27.

LOCATION   Northwestern New Mexico, in the town of Aztec. From Cortez, take U.S. 160 east to Durango, Colorado, then turn south on U.S. 550. The monument headquarters is near the junction of U.S. 550 and New Mexico 44.

ACCESS   The ruins are reached by a three-hundred-yard self-guiding loop trail that begins at the Visitor's Center.

FACILITIES   The monument headquarters has drinking water, restrooms, books for sale, and a small, shaded picnic area. Camping is not allowed here, but sites are available in the town of Aztec and, to the east, along the San Juan River.

INTERPRETIVE SERVICES   A limited number of guided hikes are available for large groups with advance reservations. A small but excellent collection of Anasazi artifacts is displayed in the Visitor's Center.

THE multistoried, five-hundred-room complex at Aztec is built in the shape of an E, and is situated on a tree-covered plain near the Animas River. The main ruins are completely excavated and many of the rooms restored, including a large kiva in the plaza. Construction at the site was begun about A.D. 1110 and was completed in 1125. Here, as at Salmon (see also *Salmon Ruins*), inhabitants of Chaco Canyon were transplanted—about 450 of them at the pueblo's peak occupation. They were farmers, irrigating their fields from the permanent water supply of the Animas River, and probably sending much of the agriculture produced to Chaco Canyon. Their tenure at the Aztec site lasted about a hundred years.

In 1225 or 1230 the pueblo was reoccupied, this time by Mesa Verde Anasazi, who in the span of a few years remodeled the town and built several new dwellings of their own. Compared to the previous masonry, however, their work was shoddy. The Mesa Verdeans remained until sometime between 1276 and 1300. The dwellings were then abandoned forever.

The first non-Indian to visit the ruins was a government geologist who surveyed portions of the San Juan Basin in 1859. During the succeeding years the area was settled by ranchers and farmers; many sealed rooms in Aztec were breached by these local residents, and many artifacts removed. In 1916 the pueblo was excavated by the American Museum of Natural History. The museum later purchased the site and donated it to the federal government. Official monument status was bestowed in 1923.

The remarkable element at Aztec, as at Salmon Ruins to the west, is the construction. The masonry was done mostly by women and, considering the primitive tools, the work is astonishing. Sandstone was carried in from a distant quarry, then after being shaped with stone tools was laid with precision into mud mortar. The work must have been backbreaking, but the result— snug, weatherproof homes that were cool in the summer and warm in winter—was worth the effort. The Chacoans were probably the finest Anasazi masons in the Southwest.

17 Mesa Verde National Park

A N A S A Z I

HOURS Park Entrance Road, 24 hours. Ruins Road Drive, 8 A.M. – sunset. Archaeological Museum: summer, 8 A.M. – 6:30 P.M. daily; winter, 8 A.M. – 5 P.M. daily. *Hours are subject to change without notice depending upon weather conditions and public-use intensity.*

ELEVATION 7000 feet.

ACRES 53,000.

LOCATION From Cortez, take U.S. 160 east about 10 miles to the Park Entrance Road. Far View Visitor's Center is 15 miles into the park from this junction; the Archaeological Museum and the major ruins are about 21 miles.

The Park Entrance Road is paved but extremely narrow and winding. Traffic during the summer months may be heavy, so allow at least 45 minutes from the U.S. 160 junction to the museum. During the winter, the road may be closed for short periods owing to snow or rockslide.

Cliff Palace—the greatest of Mesa Verde's canyon cities.

MESA Verde straddles a series of fingerlike, pine- and pinon-covered mesas, each separated by deep, narrow canyons. The park is a showcase of Anasazi culture, with nearly 4000 dwellings and the finest public display of Anasazi tools, implements, pottery, and day-to-day necessities in the Southwest. Here lie examples from almost every stage of Anasazi development—from early Basketmaker pithouses to mesa-top, apartment-style pueblos to sprawling cliff cities built in the final, desperate days of their civilization.

Humans first occupied Mesa Verde only midway through the sixth century after Christ, although they had resided in the surrounding flatlands for several thousand years. Why this lush mesa country was not utilized before is a mystery. Perhaps it was simply too rugged for early man's tastes.

By A.D. 600, Basketmaker Anasazi were living in single-family underground pithouses on the mesa tops and were farming small plots of beans and semidomesticated grain plants. They used very primitive pottery and hunted with the *atlatl* ("spear thrower"). Probably, they depended heavily upon tubers, wild berries and nuts, and insects as diet supplements.

Two hundred years later, the people had abandoned their pithouses and were living in small, compact, above-ground villages. The bow and arrow were in use for hunting, but with corn, squash, and melons added to the diet of beans, agriculture was the primary means of subsistence. The mesas were ideal for farming, with long growing seasons, hot summer temperatures, fertile soils, and dependable late-summer rains. Winters were relatively mild but wet enough to prepare the ground adequately for spring planting. As added insurance, check dams and small reservoirs had been constructed to trap and hold rain runoff.

Both dogs and turkeys had been domesticated at Mesa Verde by about A.D. 900, but neither species was utilized much for food in this particular community. Dogs were kept as sentries, pack animals, and sources of fur; turkey feathers were stripped of their herl, and this fluffy material was wound about

ACCESS In the summer months, guided tours are scheduled several times a day to three of the largest cliff ruins—Balcony House, Spruce Tree House, and Cliff Palace. Many other ruins can be viewed from overlooks along Ruins Road Drive. Also, from June to September bus tours leave every half hour from Far View Visitor's Center to Wetherill Mesa Ruins complex, a less developed group of Anasazi dwellings in the western portion of the park. (Private cars are not allowed on the Wetherill Mesa road.) Bus tours last four hours; the first tour leaves at 9 A.M., the final tour daily at 3 P.M.

During the winter, the park grounds can be used, but among the structures only the Archaeological Museum, Visitor's Center, Spruce Tree House Ruin, and a few mesa-top dwellings are open to the public.

Because times and dates for scheduled tours as well as for overall use of the park are subject to change, before leaving Cortez be sure to inquire by telephone about what is open and what is closed.

BACKCOUNTRY Day hiking only is permitted, and on only three trails in the ruins area—Pictograph Point Trail, Spruce Canyon Trail, and Soda Canyon Overlook. Each is less than three miles in length. For information, maps, and permits, inquire at the Chief Ranger's office near the Archaeological Museum.

plant-fiber cords. The insulated cords were then carefully woven into blankets and capes.

By 1150, perhaps 5000 people lived atop Mesa Verde. The simple one-story villages had disappeared, replaced by sprawling, multistoried two- to three-hundred–room apartment houses. The range of the culture itself had been extended as well, influencing other Anasazi communities within a hundred-mile radius in the arts, farming techniques, and building methods.

Food was in surplus, and the people had time to do other things. The potters had become prolific and talented; almost every type of bowl, mug, pitcher, and ladle imaginable was in daily use. The art of weaving had been acquired too, and large quantities of cotton were coming into the area by trade. Here was a true golden age—a time of plenty. It was not to last long.

Less than a century later, some type of upheaval shook the population of Mesa Verde, and a major lifestyle change took place. Perhaps enemies had invaded the mesa; perhaps a large, hungry community, faced with deepening drought conditions, had been divided by squabbles over food or water access or religious beliefs. Perhaps increasingly cold weather had made habitation on the unprotected mesa tops uncomfortable. Perhaps it was a combination of all these or none at all. Whatever happened, the massive mesa-top homes were abandoned in favor of new towns constructed in canyon-side caves and amphitheaters.

The thirteenth-century move from mesa top to canyon cave must have been difficult for the Anasazi. Each of the millions of building stones had to be carried into the canyon by hand. Most of these new towns had no water nearby, so water for both drinking and for use in building mortar was also carried in. In return for their trouble, the people of Mesa Verde could feel secure, at least from human enemies. Only direct frontal attacks could have been launched on most of the towns, and even then the attacker would have been down a steep slope from his target.

In the new towns, however, many fields went untended, and the boundaries of others were reduced. Then, in 1275 or 1276, rainfall on Mesa Verde ceased entirely. Perhaps that was the last straw. At least from the standpoint of cultural preservation, the Mesa Verde people's lifestyle changes were unsuccessful. They migrated elsewhere, probably in numerous small groups. By 1300, about the time the rains started again, Mesa Verde was deserted.

The ruins were likely visited by prospectors in the 1870s, but in 1874 photographer William Henry Jackson was the first white man to officially

Bicycling in the park is encouraged, although you must stay on designated roads. Cross-country skiing now also is encouraged (after many years of prohibition), but permits are required. Inquire at the Chief Ranger's office.

FACILITIES   Drinking water, restrooms, and telephones are available and books and gifts are for sale at the Archaeological Museum. Gasoline, lodging, and meals are available at the Far View Visitor's Center and the adjacent Far View Lodge. The park has a four-hundred–site modern campground with hookups and sanitary dump at Morefield, four miles from the park entrance; it offers Indian arts and crafts, groceries, lunches, camper supplies, gas, and a laundromat. Reservations are not required, but in midsummer they would be a good idea. Two picnic areas are available in the park, one at the Archaeological Museum, the other along Ruins Road Drive. *In winter, no gas, food, or lodging is available in the park.*

INTERPRETIVE SERVICES   Both Far View Visitor's Center and the Archaeological Museum display excellent collections of Anasazi artifacts. From June to September, campfire programs are given nightly at Morefield Campground, beginning at 9 P.M.

Square Tower House.

record sight of the dwellings in the area. Between 1881 and 1887, several small Mesa Verde outliers were discovered; but not until 1888, when Richard Wetherill and Charles Mason stumbled across what now is known as Spruce Tree House Ruin, was the size of the abandoned Anasazi community realized. In succeeding years, other large ruins were discovered by both the Wetherill family and area ranchers. Thousands of artifacts were removed. To protect the mesa, national park status was bestowed on June 29, 1906.

More recently, heavy visitor use, unauthorized digging, and careless trampling of sites have resulted in the National Park Service restricting unaccompanied walking tours to many of the Mesa Verde cliff dwellings. Some ruins have been closed entirely.

18 Ute Mountain Tribal Park, Mancos Canyon

A N A S A Z I

DAYS Monday through Friday, by reservation (and in the company of a Ute guide) only, as weather permits. *Tour days and times are subject to change without notice.*

ELEVATION 6500–7000 feet.

ACRES 125,000.

LOCATION From Cortez, take U.S. 666 south 20 miles to the Towaoc, Colorado, turnoff. Tours assemble at the junction of U.S. 666 and the Towaoc Road. Towaoc village (and the tribal headquarters) is 3 miles west from the highway.

ACCESS Visitors with reservations are requested to meet in front of the Ute Mountain Ute Pottery Factory at 9 A.M. on the day of their tour. Tours usually last all day. Tour members must provide their own automobiles, lunches, and drinking water. Since some hiking is involved, wear sturdy shoes, carry a canteen, and wear a hat.

BACKCOUNTRY Unaccompanied hiking is prohibited, but the park offers one- to four-day backcountry trips led by Ute guides, by reservation.

Anasazi ruin at Mancos Canyon.

SITUATED on the southern edge of Mesa Verde National Park, Mancos Canyon contains hundreds of Anasazi cliff and surface dwellings, some of them as large as any found in Mesa Verde. Here also are thousands of petroglyphs and pictographs—the art galleries of the ancients. Little excavation work has been done in Mancos Canyon, and most of the dwellings are as they were when abandoned. (However, the present-day Indians, the Ute Mountain Utes, are planning widespread development for the future.)

As part of the Mesa Verde system, the Mancos Canyon community underwent the same cultural development and decline as the people at Mesa Verde itself. (See *Mesa Verde.*)

Dwellings in Mancos Canyon are not as picture perfect as those in Mesa Verde, since most have not been excavated. The canyon country here, however, has been so little touched by modern man that visitors can view the region as it was viewed by the Anasazi a thousand years ago.

CAUTION   All roads leading into Mancos Canyon are unpaved. Some are extremely rough and narrow with high centers. Each tour is accompanied by a four-wheel-drive vehicle with towing capabilities, but visitors would be advised to bring along plenty of spare parts. Fill up with gasoline before leaving Cortez—the round-trip tour exceeds 50 miles.

FACILITIES   The canyon has no facilities except a primitive campground on the Mancos River, available by reservation. Campers will be accompanied there in the evening by a guide, and retrieved in the morning.

You will probably be taken on a lengthy and unadvertised tour of the Ute Mountain Ute Pottery Factory *before* leaving for Mancos Canyon. Frankly, Ute Mountain pottery is substandard and is not a good investment.

INTERPRETIVE SERVICES   Overnight visitors are occasionally given an introductory slide show at the campground.

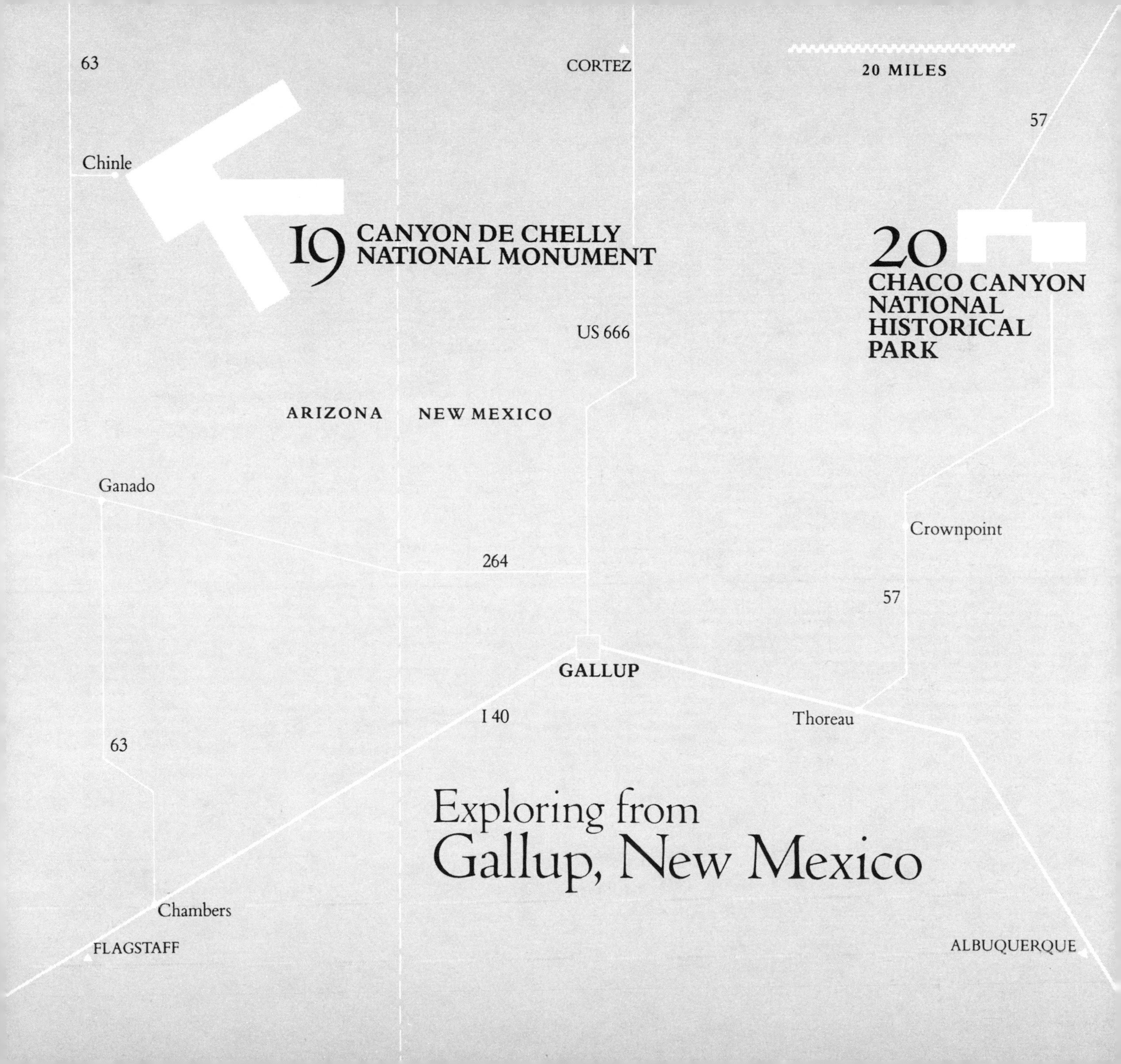
63
CORTEZ
20 MILES
57
Chinle
19 CANYON DE CHELLY NATIONAL MONUMENT
20 CHACO CANYON NATIONAL HISTORICAL PARK
US 666
ARIZONA
NEW MEXICO
Ganado
Crownpoint
264
57
GALLUP
I 40
Thoreau
63
Chambers
FLAGSTAFF
ALBUQUERQUE

Exploring from Gallup, New Mexico

19 Canyon de Chelly National Monument

A N A S A Z I

HOURS 8 A.M. – 5 P.M. daily.

ELEVATION 5400–7000 feet.

ACRES 83,000.

LOCATION From Gallup, New Mexico, take U.S. 666 north 8 miles to the State Highway 264 junction. Turn left and follow 264 about 50 miles to the Arizona 63 junction. Turn right and stay on Highway 63 to Chinle, Arizona. Turn right into Chinle, and follow the signs to monument headquarters. Alternatively from Gallup, take Interstate 40 west to the Chambers exit. Leaving the freeway, take Arizona 63 about 75 miles to Chinle.

White House Ruin.

CANYON de Chelly National Monument actually consists of three canyons—Canyon de Chelly, Canyon del Muerto, and Monument Canyon—each five hundred to seven hundred feet deep from rim to floor, and all running east to west. They meet a few miles east of Chinle. Within the canyon complex are nearly 2000 archaeological sites, of which 60 are considered major dwellings. The monument is on Navajo land, however, and only 3 sites are easily accessible to visitors. The best preserved and most spectacular of these is White House Ruin, situated 6 miles up Canyon de Chelly. There are actually two sets of dwellings here. Sixty rooms and several kivas sit upon the canyon floor adjacent to the river; 35 feet above, perched in a cliff-face alcove, are 10 more rooms. Above that, the sheer cliff blossoms outward 500 feet to meet the sky. Built about A.D. 1060 and abandoned by 1275, the ruins are thought to have housed around a hundred people. Antelope House Ruin, a 50-room, multistoried village occupied from A.D. 700 until 1260, is about 5 miles up Canyon del Muerto. This ruin takes its name from the four pronghorn antelope painted on a nearby cliff by an early Navajo artist. The largest ruin in the canyon complex is Mummy Cave, 17 miles up Canyon del Muerto. Here, about 90 rooms were built in two adjacent caverns several hundred feet above the Rio del Muerto ("River of the Dead"); this site was occupied from about 300 until 1300. In this monument, Mummy Cave is the dwelling continually inhabited the longest. It may have been a refuge for migrating Anasazi clans attempting to escape the thirteenth-century drought. Its name comes from the discovery in the late 1800s of two mummified Anasazi in a talus slope below the ruin.

Human occupation of Canyon de Chelly began shortly after the time of Christ, when Basketmaker Anasazi moved into the canyon caves. Agriculture arrived here early; by A.D. 300, corn and beans were primary sources of food. Hunting and gathering were still practiced but were probably secondary to farming activities, at least during the growing season.

ACCESS   The north rim of Canyon del Muerto and the south rim of Canyon de Chelly are skirted by well-maintained roads. Numerous overlooks give good views of the canyons as well as of many of the larger ruins.

White House Ruin can be reached by a 2.5-mile (round trip) trail that begins at the White House Overlook on South Rim Drive. The trail starts about 150 yards east of the parking lot (on the right, as you face the canyon). The hike is strenuous, descending 500 feet to the canyon floor, so carry drinking water and wear sturdy shoes.

To visit all other ruins in the canyon complex, you must be accompanied by a Navajo guide or park ranger. Commercial full- or half-day jeep trips can be arranged through the monument headquarters or the Thunderbird Lodge in Chinle. If you prefer to hike, you can reach most of the major ruins by trail, but guide arrangements are still necessary; and with the exception of walks to Mummy Cave and Antelope House Ruin, the hikes are extremely strenuous. Four-hour ranger-guided hikes into the canyons leave from the Visitor's Center, generally at 8 A.M. However, they are irregularly scheduled; check at monument headquarters for times and days. No reservations are necessary; bring your own lunch and drinking water.

By 700, Anasazi lifestyles had changed considerably. Most of the canyon population had left the caves for shallow, brush-covered pithouses near the streams. Turkeys and dogs had been domesticated; cotton, probably an acquisition from Mexico, was being grown along with the corn and beans, and squash, as well.

Over the next few centuries, Canyon de Chelly's population increased substantially. New villages were started and more fields planted. Pithouses were replaced with small above-ground dwellings of wattle-and-daub-construction (vertical poles planted in the ground and covered with mud); they in turn gave way to larger, multistoried buildings constructed of stone. Cloth, jewelry, and elegant pottery were in wide use.

During the eleventh century, the Anasazi left their canyon-bottom homes and moved back into the cliffs. Perhaps human enemies were about, but more likely the enemy was mother nature. Increased rainfall probably caused many canyon streams to flood, thereby washing away some of the new towns. The only escape would have been to live above the flood plain; that meant in the caves.

Slightly more than a century later, rainfall suddenly decreased. A few dwellings were abandoned by 1260, but others were occupied until 1300 or shortly thereafter. Here perhaps was a refuge where, for at least a little while, northern clans of Anasazi as well as the canyon's inhabitants took shelter.

In the following centuries, only the Hopi came to Canyon de Chelly, farming the canyon bottoms in the summer, carrying the harvest back to the Hopi mesas in the fall. Then, during the 1700s, the canyons were occupied by the Navajo, who for the next 150 years fought difficult, running battles with both the Spanish and United States armies in order to keep the land. The region today is considered the heartland of the Navajo Reservation. With permission of Navajo leaders, official monument status was bestowed in 1931.

Of the thousands of archaeological discoveries made in Canyon de Chelly, the most unusual is probably the "Burial of the Hands," in a large cave of Canyon del Muerto. Here, archaeologists discovered a pair of human arms lying side by side with their elbows touching the cave wall. Abalone-shell pendants had been wrapped around each wrist, and sandals and baskets filled with beads lay nearby. No one has yet been able to explain the reason for such a burial.

BACKCOUNTRY Overnight camping trips can be arranged through monument headquarters. Navajo guides and permits are required.

CAUTION Remember, you are on Navajo land when visiting Canyon de Chelly. Be polite, and respect the environment.

FACILITIES Drinking water, restrooms, and telephones are available and books and local Navajo crafts are for sale at monument headquarters. The monument has one campground with 95 sites, restrooms, and RV facilities. Reservations are not needed. The campground has a picnic area, but lunch on a canyon rim is far more spectacular.

INTERPRETIVE SERVICES Motoring guides for both North and South Rim drives are available upon request at the Visitor's Center, which also displays an excellent collection of Basketmaker Anasazi artifacts. Ethnology lectures are given daily, every hour or so between 10 A.M. and 2 P.M., at monument headquarters; campfire programs take place at the campground four nights a week beginning at 9 P.M. Check the information desk for the particular days. During the summer, local Navajo artists give silversmithing and weaving demonstrations in the monument headquarters lobby.

20

Chaco Culture National Historical Park

A N A S A Z I

HOURS   Summer, 8 A.M. – 5 P.M. daily. Winter, 8 A.M. – 4:30 P.M. daily.

ELEVATION   6100 feet.

ACRES   33,989.

LOCATION   Northwest New Mexico; from Gallup, drive east on Interstate 40 to the Thoreau exit. Leave the freeway and turn north on New Mexico 57. Stay on 57 to the park entrance, keeping a sharp lookout for direction signs and Navajo sheep. The last 30 miles of this road are unpaved and *usually impassable in wet weather.*

ACCESS   All major excavated ruins in Chaco Canyon can be reached by an unpaved road leading north from the Visitor's Center. Short hiking trails wind through the ruins themselves. None are strenuous.

Kin Kletso Ruin.

O F all the Anasazi communities in the American Southwest, Chaco Canyon has received the most attention. It has become, in essence, an archaeological school for the study of prehistoric American man. Twenty miles in length, three hundred feet deep, and .75-mile wide, Chaco Canyon is desert—an amalgamation of gray sand, wild grass, a few clinging shrubs, and tumbled piles of sandstone and shale—all whipped constantly by the wind. This is an unpropitious site for what was probably the largest Anasazi community in the Southwest, but scattered up and down the canyon's length along the river and on the mesa tops are the remains of nearly two thousand prehistoric dwellings. Most are little more than piles of rubble covered with ten centuries of blowing dust; however, half a dozen of the largest have been excavated and at least partially restored.

By A.D. 600 Chaco Canyon was occupied by large groups of Basketmaker Anasazi—pithouse-dwelling farmers who irrigated crops of corn with runoff from aperiodic desert storms. Two centuries later the Pueblo Period had begun and the people had left their pithouses, living instead in compact, one-story dwellings mostly clustered together near springs or other permanent sources of water.

Because of the permanent water supply and the farmland available in the Chaco area, immigrants arrived daily, and as populations grew, so did the villages. By 950 a great construction boom was underway in the canyon, and within a century most of the great Chaco pueblos had been completed. Some were more than four stories high; others contained at least eight hundred rooms. One, Pueblo Bonito, was probably the largest single building in the Southwest at the time of its construction; it is thought to have housed a thousand people.

The community at its peak was the New York City of the Southwest and the literal hub of a prehistoric wheel of civilization, its imprint still visibly spreads across miles of desert in the wheel configuration. Perhaps four thousand people lived within the canyon proper and another twenty thousand resided in

Pueblo Bonito—the largest single building in the Southwest at the time of its construction.

outlying but culturally attached towns and villages. Looking at the canyon today, it is difficult to imagine how such an arid environment supported so many people. Scientists think, however, that Chaco was not always so barren. More than one hundred thousand large trees, for example, were cut for room supports during construction of the pueblos. This means a forest was nearby—perhaps in the canyon itself, perhaps upon the mesas to either side. And since a farming operation capable of feeding four thousand people at least in part demands an enormous amount of moisture (not to mention the drinking-water requirement of that population), the now-dry river in Chaco Canyon was probably flowing healthily then.

With such a huge population competing for the area's resources, crisis was inevitable. But here, unlike at most Anasazi communities in the Southwest, it came early—during the later years of the twelfth century. By 1150 the resources had been nearly exhausted. The prehistoric forests had been removed, branch by branch, until nothing remained for either building material or firewood. Game in the region had long since disappeared, and heavy and continuous foot traffic had badly eroded the earth. Worse, after centuries of use the farmlands were infertile. Rainfall was decreasing, and even with the assistance of catch dams and an extensive system of water-trapping canals, the water was not sufficient to go around. Supplies from the Chaco outliers helped some (see *Salmon Ruins*), but obviously not enough. By 1175, with the exception of a small group of diehards, Chaco had been abandoned.

By the beginning of the thirteenth century, the canyon's only occupants were rattlesnakes and desert mice. Then, about A.D. 1250, some of the buildings were reoccupied by clans of Mesa Verde Anasazi, probably in search of havens from the drought and social upheaval at the great mesa to the north. These people left a century later, and the canyon lay undisturbed until groups of Navajo moved into the area in the 1700s. The first whites to visit Chaco and record their findings arrived about 1850. Major excavations took place during the late nineteenth and early twentieth centuries. Official monument status was bestowed in 1907, and Chaco became a national park in 1981.

One of the most interesting questions arising from archaeological studies at Chaco concerns the disposition of the dead. Only a few hundred small burials have been found in the canyon, in no way accounting for the thousands of people who must have died during the long occupation. Many scientists think that somewhere in the canyon lies a massive central cemetery.

Behind a group of large boulders atop Fajada Butte, in the canyon's southern end, two sets of concentric circles have been carved into the rock about a foot apart. (See also *Hovenweep National Monument.*) For years, archaeologists were puzzled by this seemingly meaningless petroglyph; then someone suggested it might be an astronomical calendar. Sure enough, during the summer solstice (about June 22) a narrow strip of light shining through a crack between the boulders perfectly bisects one set of circles. During the winter solstice (about December 22) the other circle is similarly bisected.

INTERPRETIVE SERVICES   During the summer months, at least one guided tour is offered each day. Times vary, but a schedule is posted in the Visitor's Center. Trail-guide leaflets are available for all major ruins at either park headquarters or the trailheads. Campfire programs are given each evening in the summer; times are posted in the Visitor's Center. An excellent museum displays many Chacoan culture artifacts.

East wall of Kin Kletso Ruin.

Exploring from Albuquerque, New Mexico

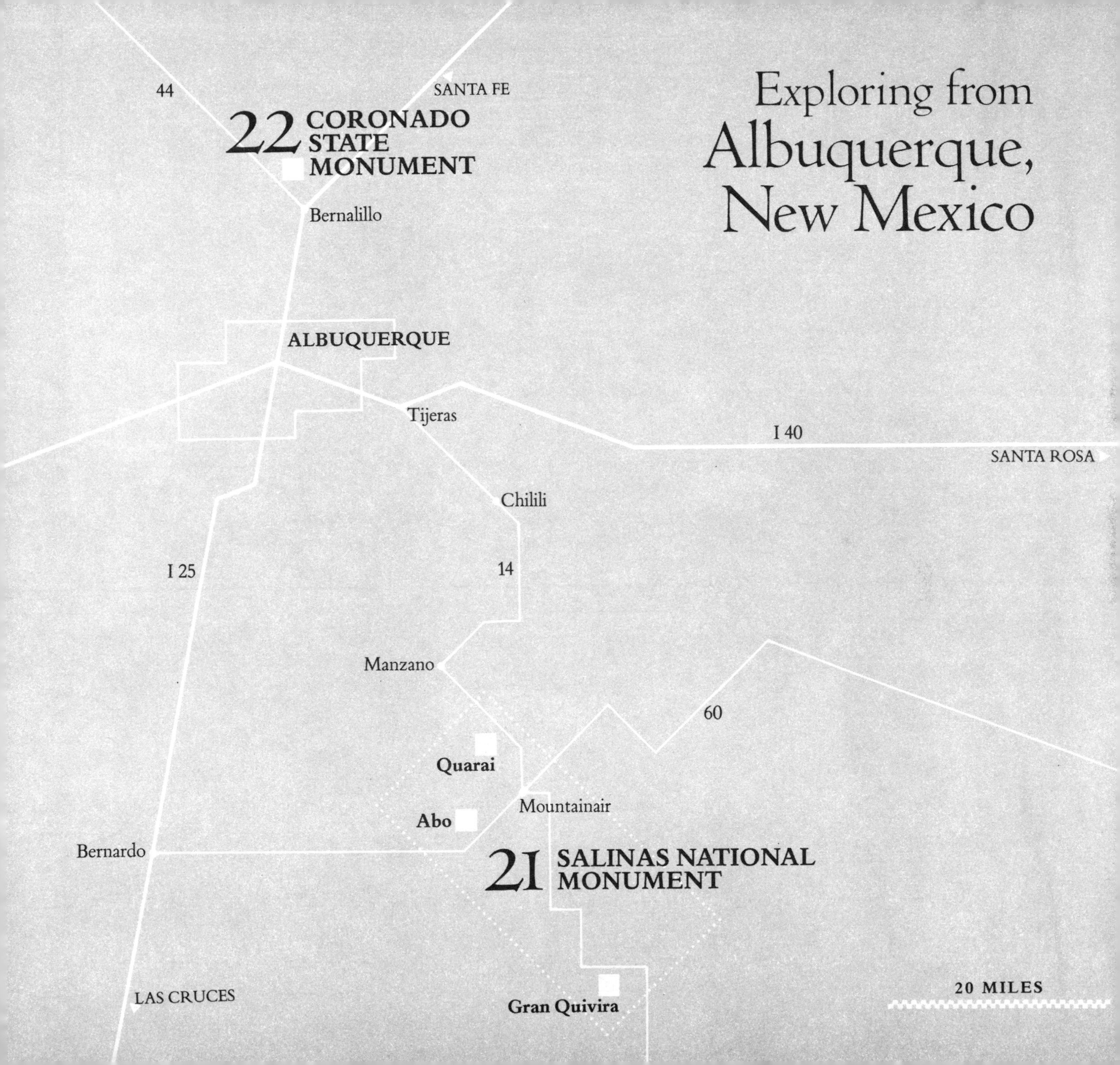
44
SANTA FE
22 CORONADO STATE MONUMENT
Bernalillo
ALBUQUERQUE
Tijeras
I 40
SANTA ROSA
Chilili
I 25
14
Manzano
60
Quarai
Mountainair
Abo
Bernardo
21 SALINAS NATIONAL MONUMENT
20 MILES
LAS CRUCES
Gran Quivira

Salinas National Monument

MOGOLLON / ANASAZI

HOURS   Summer, 8 A.M. – 7 P.M. daily. Winter, 8 A.M. – 5 P.M. daily.

ELEVATION   6000–6300 feet.

ACRES   1077.

LOCATION   To reach the Abo Unit from Albuquerque, take Interstate 25 to the Bernardo exit. Leave the freeway and follow U.S. 60 east 26 miles to the monument entrance. To reach the Gran Quivira Unit, follow U.S. 60 east 13 miles past Abo to the New Mexico 14 junction. Turn south (right) on N.M. 14; the monument entrance road is 26 miles farther. To reach the Quarai Unit, proceed to the N.M. 14 junction as for Gran Quivira, but turn north (left) on N.M. 14 and travel about 8 miles to the monument entrance.

Quarai Ruins.

THE Salinas National Monument comprises three separate units. The Abo unit consists of six large, unexcavated Indian "house mounds" (archaeologese for "pueblo units"), a central plaza, prehistoric fields, and several petroglyph sites. Also here are the ruins of the San Gregorio de Abo mission, a seventeenth-century Franciscan church. Only the church has been fully excavated.

The Gran Quivira Unit, one of the largest Anasazi ruins in New Mexico, has 21 major Indian house mounds, 10 kivas, numerous pithouses and the remains of two seventeenth-century Franciscan missions. Five kivas, 300 rooms in two of the house mounds, and one of the missions have been excavated.

Probably the most spectacular of the Southwestern Spanish missions—the one called Nuestra Señora de la Concepción—is found at Quarai. Here also are nine unexcavated Indian house mounds, two plazas, and several petroglyph sites.

Little is known of the Indian occupation of Quarai and Abo, since neither have been excavated, but Gran Quivira prehistory generally applies to the entire Salinas Valley region.

About A.D. 800, elements of the Mogollon culture moved in from the south (probably Mexico) with people who built small pithouse villages near the few natural springs in the Salinas Valley. Two hundred years later Anasazi influence began to seep into the region, and by 1100 the two cultures had blended. The Pueblo Period had started; 11 major pueblos had been constructed in the Salinas Valley, all within one or two days' journey of the others.

During the mid-sixteenth century, another influence moved into the region; whether it was Hohokam, more Anasazi, or some totally new and as yet undiscovered culture archaeologists are still unsure. Whoever the new people were, they too were absorbed into the Anasazi-Mogollon melting pot. There is no evidence to suggest that strife or warfare occurred among these three peoples.

All three units in Salinas National Monument have short, unstrenuous, self-guiding trails. To walk the longest—at Gran Quivira—requires about 30 minutes, round trip.

FACILITIES Only Gran Quivira and Quarai have modern facilities; both offer drinking water and restrooms, and sell books. Abo has no conviences of any kind. None of the sites allows camping, but all three have small picnic areas.

INTERPRETIVE SERVICES Guided hikes are available on a limited basis at Gran Quivira; trail-guide leaflets and bilingual (Spanish-English) trail signs can be found at Abo and Quarai. The Gran Quivira and Quarai sites have small exhibit centers.

In 1598, 58 years after the Coronado exploratory expedition into the Southwest (see *Coronado State Monument*), Gran Quivira was visited by Don Juan de Oñate, governor of New Mexico. He was the first European the Indians had ever seen. After his visit, missionary work quickly began, and by 1630 massive Franciscan missions had been built at Gran Quivira, Abo, and Quarai. Indian religions and ceremonies were prohibited; and the new religious activity was intense and demanding. The Indians were not asked but were required to become Christians.

The missions at Abo, Gran Quivira, and Quarai were constructed with Indian labor and were extremely costly to the Spanish crown. Interestingly enough, the governor of New Mexico wanted King Philip III of Spain to abandon the entire province, since gold and silver had not been found and the Spanish presence was costing Spain a fortune. It was the Pope, however, who had originally given the job of Christianizing the Indians to King Philip. Regardless of expense, religious activity in New Mexico was to continue—by Papal decree.

This religious fervor contributed much to both Indian and Spanish downfall in the Salinas Valley. The area was dry and produced only a small surplus of food—certainly not enough to provide both the Spanish and Indians with agricultural products. From 1666 to 1670, a severe drought occurred in the region, making things worse. (The great drought of 1276 to 1299 seems to have had little affect here.) In addition, mounted Apache raiders continually harassed the pueblos, killing warriors and stealing food. By 1677, all 11 Salinas Valley Indian towns had been abandoned, their inhabitants probably joining Rio Grande River pueblos. With no one to convert, the Spanish returned to Santa Fe, leaving their great missions to be devoured by the wind.

Abo Ruins.

22 Coronado State Monument, Kuaua Pueblo

ANASAZI / MOGOLLON

HOURS   9 A.M. – 5 P.M. Closed Tuesdays, Wednesdays, and holidays.

ELEVATION   5100 feet.

ACRES   345.

LOCATION   Central New Mexico, 18 miles north of Albuquerque. Take Interstate 25 north to the junction of New Mexico 44 (the second Bernalillo exit). Follow N.M. 44 west 1.6 miles; the monument entrance road is on the right.

ACCESS   A short, self-guiding loop trail beginning at the Visitor's Center winds through the excavated portions of the ruins complex.

FACILITIES   The monument headquarters offers drinking water, restrooms, and a gift shop. A large campground and picnic area are near N.M. 44, just off the monument entrance road; reservations are not needed.

Reconstructed kiva at Kuaua Pueblo is overshadowed by the Sandia Mountains.

THIS extensive but little-maintained ruin sits atop a sandy bluff overlooking the Rio Grande River. About .25 mile in length and nearly half that wide, Kuaua Pueblo was one of the largest ruins in the Southwest before erosion destroyed many of its outlying sections. When occupied, Kuaua contained an estimated one thousand ground-floor rooms (plus an undetermined number of upper-story rooms) arranged around several large plazas. Most of the house walls were built of soft, adobe-mud bricks. One kiva has been restored.

From whence the inhabitants of Kuaua originated, no one is sure, but the pueblo was occupied by A.D. 1300 and was probably the home of Anasazi and Mogollon drought survivors. One of 12 similar pueblos along the Rio Grande River, Kuaua was the northernmost and probably the largest. Its people were farmers, growing crops of cotton, tobacco, corn, beans, squash, and melons in large, irrigated plots along the river. Strangely enough, although an extensive system of canals brought water from the Rio Grande to the fields, the watering itself was done by hand from large pots, probably because of some religious belief.

At its peak occupation, the pueblo housed between fifteen hundred and three thousand people. In 1540, Spanish explorer Francisco Vásquez de Coronado and a large group of soldiers and Mexican Indians reached the Rio Grande Valley and wintered near the town, in the process claiming all the nearby pueblos as property of the Spanish king. Coronado, however, was overextended; his expedition was on the point of starvation. In anger, frustration, or need, the Spanish killed some of the Kuaua Indians. Others were tortured in an attempt to make them divulge the whereabouts of legendary hoards of gold and silver supposed to exist in the area. All the violence was to no avail; and not long after Coronado returned to Mexico and then to Spain, where he was tried for his maltreatment of the Indians.

Between the time Coronado left and the year 1598, Kuaua was gutted by fire, and the pueblo was abandoned, its occupants probably joining the

INTERPRETIVE SERVICES Occasional guided hikes are given to educational groups with advance reservations. The ruins trail is well marked with bilingual (Spanish-English) information signs, but no trail-guide leaflets are available. A large exhibit center offers an informative glimpse into pueblo life, both ancient and contemporary.

Kiva murals at Kuaua Pueblo.

nearby towns of Santa Ana and Sandia. For centuries the pueblo lay unbothered, its walls eroding in the wind. In 1934, archaeologists from the Museum of New Mexico, the University of New Mexico, and the School of American Research began joint excavations of the site. It was designated as a state monument in 1940.

Digging into a large, square, rubble-filled kiva in 1935, archaeologists made an astounding discovery. There on the interior walls was a nearly intact set of red, yellow, black, white, and bluish green paintings. Almost life-size, the "Kuaua Murals," as they have come to be called, were of masked dancers and were probably religious in nature. They can be seen in their original form in the Special Exhibit room at the monument.

20 MILES

TAOS

285

Exploring from
Santa Fe,
New Mexico

Española

5   30

25 **PUYE CLIFF DWELLINGS**

4

Los Alamos   Pojoaque

Tsankawi Ruin

4

White Rock

SANTA FE

24 **BANDELIER NATIONAL MONUMENT**

85

Glorieta   Pecos

50   **23** **PECOS NATIONAL MONUMENT**

I 25   63

DENVER

ALBUQUERQUE

23

Pecos National Monument

A N A S A Z I

HOURS Summer, 8 A.M. – 7 P.M. daily. Winter, 8 A.M. – 5 P.M. daily. Closed on Christmas.

ELEVATION 6900 feet.

ACRES 340.

LOCATION North-central New Mexico, 25 miles east of Santa Fe. Take Interstate 25 to the Glorieta exit and, leaving the freeway, follow the signs to the village of Pecos, on New Mexico 50. Then turn right onto New Mexico 63; monument headquarters is about 2 miles farther.

ACCESS A self-guiding trail winds through the monument, beginning and ending at the mission. The .75-mile loop can easily be walked in an hour.

FACILITIES At monument headquarters, books are for sale and drinking water, telephone, and restrooms are available. A small picnic area is adjacent to the Visitor's Center. Camping is not allowed.

The ruined Spanish mission at Pecos.

THE multifaceted Pecos ruin of clay, indigenous stone, and adobe mud straddles a low, grass-covered ridge in the piñon- and juniper-dotted foothills of the Sangre de Cristo ("Blood of Christ") mountains. Unexcavated house mounds at the monument's north end are the remnants of a five-story pueblo that once housed an estimated twenty-five hundred people. The only excavated ruins at the site are those of a Spanish mission and a small pueblo probably constructed in the fifteenth century. Both are adjacent to monument headquarters.

Around A.D. 1100, Anasazi farmers from the Rio Grande River pueblos moved eastward into the present-day Pecos Valley. By 1500 Pecos Pueblo, then known by its Anasazi name "Cicuyé" (which has no English translation) had been completed and was fully occupied. Extensive fields in the surrounding valley furnished the people with corn and beans; the nearby mountains were replete with wild game.

The town was first visited by Europeans in 1541, when conquistadores under the command of Spanish explorer Francisco Vásquez de Coronado passed that way in search of treasure. By the early seventeenth century, as a direct result of the first visit, Spanish priests had taken up residence at Cicuyé in an attempt to Christianize the Indians. The pueblo's name had been changed to Pecos, and a great church, the Misión de Nuestra Señora de los Angeles de Porcinúcula, had been built.

In the Pueblo Revolt of 1680, New Mexico Indians rose up against their Spanish masters, killing many and driving the remainder to El Paso, Texas. The original mission was partially demolished in the revolt, but when the Spanish returned, the mission was rebuilt. The downfall of the pueblo had begun, however. During the eighteenth century, Pecos was continually attacked by marauding Plains Indians, and in 1781 many of its inhabitants were wiped out by epidemic smallpox introduced unknowingly by the Spanish. In 1838, the last 17 survivors abandoned the town and moved across the Rio Grande River to live with relatives in the Indian village of Jemez.

Not quite a century passed before excavations of the ruins and mission began, directed by one of the world's most famous archaeologists, Alfred Kidder. Official monument status was bestowed in 1965.

At the Pecos monument, the mission is an architectural wonder. In some places its adobe walls are seven feet thick, and the roof timbers weigh several tons. It was, in fact, a fortress, perhaps built as a reminder to the Indians that God and the Catholic Church were invincible. Here, as elsewhere in the New Mexico pueblos, the Indians were forced to become Christians. All forms of Indian religion were quashed.

INTERPRETIVE SERVICES   By advance reservation, guided tours are arranged for large groups. A small museum in the Visitor's Center displays Anasazi and Spanish artifacts recovered from the ruins. During the summer, the National Park Service sponsors daily demonstrations of Indian arts and crafts at the monument. Many participants in the demonstrations are descendants (now from Jemez Pueblo) of original Cicuyé inhabitants. Demonstrations include pottery making, bread baking, basket weaving, and the creation of turkey-feather blankets.

Contemporary Southwest Indian pottery with ancient design motifs.

24

Bandelier National Monument

HOURS Summer, 8 A.M. – 6 P.M. daily. Winter, 8 A.M. – 5 P.M. daily. Closed on Christmas.

ELEVATION 6066 feet.

ACRES 32,000.

LOCATION North-central New Mexico, 43 miles west of Santa Fe. Take U.S. 285 north 15 miles to Pojoaque and turn left (west) onto New Mexico 4; the monument entrance is 28 miles beyond. Just off New Mexico 4 and only 13 miles from the U.S. 285 junction is the pullout giving access to a detached portion of Bandelier, Tsankawi Ruin.

Restored dwelling at Bandelier National Monument.

BANDELIER National Monument is a part of the Pajarito Plateau, a canyon-slashed basalt mesa that juts eastward from the slopes of the Jemez Mountains. Hundreds of prehistoric dwellings have been built upon the plateau; three of these—Tyuonyi Ruin, Long House Ruin, and Tsankawi Ruin—are easily accessible to visitors.

Tyuonyi Ruin is a circular, four-tiered pueblo of about four hundred rooms that rises from the bottom of Frijoles Canyon, one of the Pajarito Plateau's largest volcanic chasms. The ground floor, all that remains of this once-multistoried town, has been totally excavated. At peak occupation, Tyuonyi housed an estimated hundred people.

Just up the canyon from Tyuonyi is Long House Ruin, a partially excavated, oblong dwelling of two hundred rooms, built adjacent to the southwest-facing wall of Frijoles. Originally two or three stories high, Long House was attached to the cliff face itself; secondary "cave rooms" were cut by Anasazi masons into the soft, volcanic tuff. At peak occupation perhaps 75 people lived here.

Tsankawi Ruin, a detached portion of Bandelier, is an unexcavated, roughly rectangular 350-room pueblo straddling a volcanic mesa on the eastern edge of Pajarito Plateau. This town, too, was once multistoried, and it probably housed two hundred people. However, Tsankawi is the least explored of the three major Bandelier sites; it has not been excavated, and little is known about its prehistoric occupation.

Not until the late twelfth century was the Pajarito Plateau occupied, by groups of Anasazi migrating from the west. Once they had arrived, however, they were quick to settle, building hundreds of small dwellings across the plateau's rugged lava and cactus landscape. Near most of the dwellings were tiny farms from which the Anasazi gleaned their meager but adequate living.

During the late 1300s, perhaps for defensive purposes, these small agricultural units began to consolidate, and by 1450 most plateau inhabitants were congregated in several large pueblos. The fields in the nearby rich canyon bot-

ACCESS   Self-guiding trails, originating at monument headquarters, lead to all ruins in the immediate Frijoles Canyon area. None are more than two miles in length, but occasional climbing is necessary, especially along those sections of trail that follow the original Indian pathways. Comfortable shoes and a canteen of water will make the trails seem less strenuous.

The trail to Tsankawi Ruin begins at a roadside pullout on New Mexico 4, described above. The round trip to the main ruin is about 2 miles and requires several steep climbs. Summer visitors should carry water.

BACKCOUNTRY   Bandelier is a backpacker's delight. More than 65 miles of maintained trails crisscross its 32,000 acres, leading to unexcavated wilderness ruins, spectacular vistas, and solitary campsites. Round trip from the Visitor's Center, the five major Bandelier trails vary in length from 5 miles to 22. However, the country is rough and unforgiving. Hikers should be in good physical condition and have trail-tried equipment. Horseback trips are encouraged, but no animals are available locally. The required backcountry permit can be obtained at the Visitor's Center.

FACILITIES   The monument headquarters offers drinking water, restrooms, telephone, curio shop, snack bar, books for sale, and a small grocery store. Cottonwood Picnic Area provides handy, shaded lunch spots along Frijoles Creek. Ponderosa Campground (for family units and by reservation only) and Juniper Campground provide tables, fireplaces, restrooms, and sanitary dump stations. No RV hookups are available.

INTERPRETIVE SERVICES   Ranger-guided group hikes are by reservation only, but ethnobotany walks and campfire programs are given each day during the summer (check the information desk for times and days). Trail-guide leaflets are available for all three major ruins at monument headquarters and at the trailheads themselves. Foreign-language leaflets are available in French, German, Japanese, and Spanish. An exhibit room offers a natural-history and photographic gallery, introductory slide show, and excellent examples of Anasazi artifacts.

toms were larger, and were irrigated in dry weather by primitive canal systems. Game was thick in the canyon country, and the weather mild. Existence was perhaps slightly crowded in the narrow canyon but probably comfortable.

Less than a century later, communal life on Pajarito Plateau suddenly ended. Sometime between 1500 and 1550, the Anasazi settlements were abandoned. Whether occupation of the plateau was ended by one large migration or many small ones is unknown. It is thought, however, that the Anasazi did not go far. Modern Indian pueblos along the nearby Rio Grande River claim descent from these early plateau dwellers.

The plateau was first explored by Europeans between 1595 and 1598, but little interest in the region was shown until the eighteenth century, when Spanish settlers petitioned land in the area from the Spanish crown. (New Mexico was a Spanish province until 1821.) Even then, the great ruins were ignored except as a source of stones for building walls and farm fences. Anthropologist Adolph Bandelier (for whom the monument is named) began explorations of the ruins in 1880, but major excavations did not occur until the early 1900s. Official monument status was bestowed in 1916.

A mile north of the Frijoles Canyon Visitor's Center, 140 feet above the canyon floor, is a shallow overhang in the tuff cliff known as Ceremonial Cave. This was once the home of an Anasazi clan or several small families. Views from Ceremonial Cave of Frijoles Canyon are stupendous, and the climb up (by ladder) is well worth the effort.

Also noteworthy at the monument is the art of the prolific Bandelier Anasazi. Decorating the canyon walls throughout the ruins area are hundreds of elaborate petroglyphs. And inside many of the Long House cave rooms, the walls have been literally covered with pictographs—Indian wallpaper, perhaps, to reduce the monotony.

The remains of Tyuonyi Ruin, once a large Frijoles Canyon city.

25 Puye Cliff Dwellings

ANASAZI

HOURS 8 A.M. – 6 P.M. daily, April 1 through October 31.

ELEVATION 6500 feet.

ACRES 300.

LOCATION North-central New Mexico; the ruins are on the Santa Clara Indian Reservation portion of the Pajarito Plateau. From Santa Fe take U.S. 285 north to Pojoaque and turn west on New Mexico 4; at the junction with New Mexico 30 (just across the Rio Grande River) turn north (right). Follow N.M. 30 about five miles to the Puye entrance road. The ruins are nine miles up Santa Clara Canyon.

Roof beam support holes and cave rooms in the lower ruin at Puye.

PUYE has two aggregations of dwellings, both overlooking the Pajarito Plateau and Santa Clara Canyon. High on the south-facing canyon slope is a crumbled cliff village that once was three stories high. Many of the exterior buildings were connected to cave rooms, those hand-carved into the soft tuff cliff. Only a few of the buildings have been restored. Directly above the cliff village is Top House Ruin, a two-thousand–room, partially excavated pueblo built around a large central plaza. Several mid-ruin sections have been restored.

Tree-ring dating of Top House roof timbers suggests that Puye was constructed between A.D. 1450 and 1475 by members of the same Anasazi culture that built Tsankawi, Tyuonyi, and Long House pueblos at Bandelier National Monument. (See also *Bandelier National Monument*.) Puye reached its peak occupation in about 1540. The cliff village and Top House were probably occupied at the same time, the lower section used as winter quarters, the upper for summer living. As at the towns of Bandelier, however, the occupation span at Puye was short. The Anasazi left in about 1550. The dates are speculative for both Puye and Bandelier, but they seem likely to have been abandoned at the same time.

The Santa Clara Indians, who now own the land upon which Puye sits, claim they are descended from the Pajarito Plateau Anasazi, and probably the assumption is correct. However, other Indian pueblos along the Rio Grande also display aspects of Puye culture, as do the Hopi Mesas in Arizona. And strangely enough the living Indians closest in physical type to the original Puye Anasazi (as determined with mummified remains) are the Tarahumara of northern Mexico.

The best time to visit Puye is during the Puye Ceremonial, held annually at the site in the latter part of July. The festivities include a large arts and crafts display and two days of dancing by local Indian tribes.

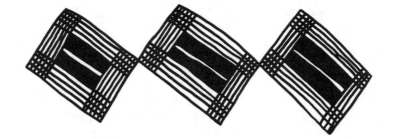

ACCESS   Several short, steep trails lead to the cliff village from the caretaker's house and parking area at the bottom of Santa Clara Canyon. Top House Ruin can be reached by trail and also by an unpaved road from the parking area. The cliff trails are strenuous.

FACILITIES   Drinking water and restrooms only are available at the caretaker's house. Several large picnic areas and camping sites are scattered throughout Santa Clara Canyon.

INTERPRETIVE SERVICES   Puye brochures are available at Santa Clara Pueblo (a few miles north of the Puye turnoff on New Mexico 30) but not often at the ruins themselves. No guided hikes or trail-guide leaflets are available, but some trails display information signs.

26
GILA CLIFF DWELLINGS
NATIONAL MONUMENT

Exploring from
Las Cruces,
New Mexico

ALBUQUERQUE

Truth or Consequences

35

15

90

US 180

Silver City

San Lorenzo

Hatch

61

US 180

I 25

LAS CRUCES

I 10

Deming

TUCSON

I 10

EL PASO

20 MILES

Gila Cliff Dwellings National Monument

M O G O L L O N

SITUATED on the southern edge of the Gila Wilderness in canyon-incised high desert, these single-story cliff dwellings are probably the best preserved of any Mogollon buildings. Perched about 180 feet above the floor of a narrow, well-wooded canyon are about 40 rooms segregated into five adjacent natural caverns. The wall stones are tightly mortared indigenous Gila conglomerate (an unusual cream-colored rock); the roof timbers and wall supports are the originals. About 15 families resided here at peak occupation.

Ceramic and architectural dating of pithouses near the cliff dwellings suggest that this site was occupied by A.D. 100. These early people were farmers but depended heavily upon hunting and gathering in the nearby mountains. By A.D. 1000, however, considerable interaction had taken place between the Mogollon and the Hohokam, and Anasazi cultures from the west and north. New agricultural techniques had been introduced to the Mogollon. Tilled crops of corn and beans flourished in irrigated canyon-bottom plots and the pithouses were replaced by square or rectangular above-ground dwellings. In return, the Mogollon are speculated to have passed on the use of the bow and arrow to the Hohokam and Anasazi, by accident or intention.

Sometime in the mid-thirteenth century, the Gila cliff houses were constructed. Their occupation was short. Less than a hundred years later, they were abruptly abandoned; the reason is unknown. Apache Indians later occupied the region, followed by Spanish colonists. The first non-Indian visit to the ruins took place in the 1830s, and monument status was bestowed in 1907.

Gila today is not a spectacular ruin, as are the great Anasazi cliff houses, farther north; but if Mogollon masons were not exceptionally talented, other of their artisans were. Mogollon potters created unique and lovely black and white and reddish brown bowls, mugs, and plates that had no equal in the prehistoric Southwest. Pot hunters and collectors recognize these qualities; a single ceramic piece of the late Mogollon (known as the Mimbres) may fetch sums in excess of $15,000.

BACKCOUNTRY The nearby Gila Wilderness (America's first official Wilderness Area) has numerous hiking trails. Backpacking and day hiking are encouraged, but in this rough country equipment should be trial-tested and reliable. Few ruins exist in the backcountry, but trout fishing in the West and Middle forks of the Gila River is exceptional. *Permits are required to enter the wilderness.* Arrangements for privately guided trips can be made at Gila Hot Springs (near the monument entrance). Information and detailed maps of the wilderness are available at the Visitor's Center.

FACILITIES The monument headquarters has books for sale, drinking water, and restrooms. Here also are two improved camping areas and a picnic site. Nearby Gila Hot Springs offers groceries, gasoline, and camping and picnic supplies.

INTERPRETIVE SERVICES Limited guided tours are available with advance reservations. Trail-guide leaflets can be picked up at the Forest Service Ranger Station and the Visitor's Center. A small museum offers an excellent display of Mogollon artifacts and ceramics.

Directory of Site Headquarters

AZTEC RUINS NATIONAL MONUMENT
P.O. Box U
Aztec, New Mexico 87410
(505) 334-6174

BANDELIER NATIONAL MONUMENT
Los Alamos, New Mexico 87544
(505) 672-3861

CANYON DE CHELLY NATIONAL
MONUMENT
P.O. Box 588
Chinle, Arizona 86503
(602) 674-5436

CASA GRANDE RUINS NATIONAL
MONUMENT
Coolidge, Arizona 85228
(602) 723-3172

CHACO CULTURE NATIONAL
HISTORICAL PARK
Star Route 4, Box 6500
Bloomfield, New Mexico 87413
(505) 786-5384

CORONADO STATE MONUMENT
P.O. Box 95
Bernalillo, New Mexico 87004
(505) 867-5351

GILA CLIFF DWELLINGS NATIONAL
MONUMENT
Route 11, Box 100
Silver City, New Mexico 88061
(505) 534-9344

GLEN CANYON NATIONAL RECREATION
AREA, RAINBOW BRIDGE TRAIL
P.O. Box 1507
Page, Arizona, 86040
(602) 645-2511

GRAND GULCH PRIMITIVE AREA
Kane Gulch Ranger Station
Star Route
Blanding, Utah 84511
(no telephone)

HOVENWEEP NATIONAL MONUMENT
McElmo Route
Cortez, Colorado 81321
(no telephone)

MESA VERDE NATIONAL PARK
Mesa Verde, Colorado 81330
(303) 529-4461, 529-4475

MONTEZUMA CASTLE NATIONAL
MONUMENT
Camp Verde, Arizona 86322
(602) 567-3322

MONUMENT VALLEY NAVAJO TRIBAL
PARK
P.O. Box 93
Monument Valley, Utah 86536
(801) 727-3287

NATURAL BRIDGES NATIONAL
MONUMENT
Star Route
Blanding, Utah 84511
(801) 259-7164

NAVAJO NATIONAL MONUMENT
Tonalea, Arizona 86044
(602) 672-2366

PECOS NATIONAL MONUMENT
Drawer 11
Pecos, New Mexico 87552
(505) 757-6414

PUEBLO GRANDE RUIN
4619 E. Washington Street
Phoenix, Arizona 85034
(602) 275-3452

PUYE CLIFF DWELLINGS
Santa Clara Governor
Santa Clara Pueblo
P.O. Box 580
Espanola, New Mexico 87532
(505) 753-7326

SALINAS NATIONAL MONUMENT
P.O. Box 496
Mountainair, New Mexico 87036
(505) 847-2770

SALMON RUINS
Route 3, Box 858
Farmington, New Mexico 87401
(505) 632-2013

TONTO NATIONAL MONUMENT
P.O. Box 707
Roosevelt, Arizona 85545
(602) 467-2241

TUZIGOOT NATIONAL MONUMENT
P.O. Box 68
Clarkdale, Arizona 86324
(602) 634-5564

UTE MOUNTAIN TRIBAL PARK,
MANCOS CANYON
Towaoc, Colorado 81334
(303) 565-3751, ext. 282

WALNUT CANYON NATIONAL
MONUMENT
Route 1, Box 25
Flagstaff, Arizona 86001
(602) 526-3367

WUPATKI NATIONAL MONUMENT
Tuba Star Route
Flagstaff, Arizona 86001
(602) 774-7000

Glossary

NAME	PRONUNCIATION	ORIGIN	MEANING
ABO	ah-BOW	Unknown	Unknown
ANASAZI	awn-ah-SAW-see	Navajo	Ancient enemies
BETATAKIN	buh-TATA-kin	Navajo	Ledge house
CASA CHIQUITA	cah-sah chi-KEE-ta	Spanish	Little house
CASA GRANDE	cah-sah GRAHN-de	Spanish	Big house
CHACO	CHA-koh	Spanish corruption of Tesegi (Navajo)	Rock canyon
CHETRO KETL	che-tro kettle	Aztec	Rain house
CICUYÉ	see-COO-YAY	Anasazi	Unknown
DE CHELLY	d'SHAY	Spanish corruption of Tesegi (Navajo)	Rock canyon
FRIJOLES	free-HOLE-es	Spanish	Beans
GILA	HEE-lah	Spanish	Unknown
GRAN QUIVIRA	grahn qui-VEER-ah	Spanish	Great treasure
HOHOKAM	hoho-KAHM	Pima	Those who have gone
HOVENWEEP	HO-vin-weep	Ute	Deserted valley
HUNGO PAVI	hun-go pah-VEE	Corruption of Hopi	Place of reed spring
KEET SEEL	keet SEEL	Navajo	Broken pottery
KIN KLETSO	kin KLET-so	Navajo	Yellow house
KUAUA	kah-WAH-wah	Tewa	Evergreen
LOMAKI	lah-MAW-kee	Hopi	Beautiful house

NAME	PRONUNCIATION	ORIGIN	MEANING
MESA VERDE	MAY-suh VER-day	Spanish	Green table
MOGOLLON	muggy-OWN	Spanish	Don Juan Ignacio Flores Mogollon, Governor of New Mexico, 1712–1715
NALAKIHU	nah-LAH-kee-hoo	Hopi	House standing alone
NONNEZOSHI	non-es-OH-shee	Navajo	Rainbow turned to stone
PAJARITO	pah-ha-REE-toe	Spanish	Little bird
PECOS	PAY-cos	Keres	Little river
PUEBLO	PWEB-loe	Spanish	Village
PUEBLO ALTO	PWEB-loe AL-toe	Spanish	High village
PUEBLO BONITO	PWEB-loe bow-NEE-toe	Spanish	Beautiful village
PUEBLO DEL ARROYO	PWEB-loe del uh-ROY-yo	Spanish	Village of the gully
PUEBLO GRANDE	PWEB-loe GRAHN-de	Spanish	Big village
PUYE	poo-YAY	Tewa	Where cotton-tails assemble
QUARAI	KUAR-i	Unknown	Unknown
SALADO	sa-LAH-tho	Spanish	Salty
SALINAS	suh-LEEN-us	Spanish	Salt valley
SINAGUA	sin-AH-WAH	Spanish	Without water
TSANKAWI	SANG-COW-WEE	Tewa	Pueblo ruin above the gap of the sharp, round cactus
TUZIGOOT	two-SEE-goot	Apache	Crooked water for the channel of the Verde River

NAME	PRONUNCIATION	ORIGIN	MEANING
TYUONYI	chew-OWN-yee	Keres	Meeting place
UNA VIDA	OON-ah VEE-tah	Spanish	A life
WUKOKI	WOO-KOE-kee	Hopi	Tall house
WUPATKI	WOO-POT-kee	Hopi	Tall house

For Further Reading

ANASAZI: ANCIENT PEOPLE OF THE ROCK. Donald G. Pike and David Muench. Palo Alto: American West Publishing Company, 1974.

ANASAZI, THE. J. Richard Ambler. Museum of Northern Arizona, 1977.

ANASAZI COMMUNITIES OF THE SAN JUAN BASIN. Marshall, Stein, Loose, and Novotny. Albuquerque: Public Service Company of New Mexico, 1979.

AMERICA B.C. Barry Fell. New York: Pocket Books, 1976.

ANCIENT MAN IN NORTH AMERICA. H.M. Wormington. Denver: Denver Museum of Natural History.

ART OF A VANISHED RACE: THE MIMBRES CLASSIC BLACK-ON-WHITE. Victor M. Giammattei, D.V.M., and Nanci Greer Reichert. Woodlands, California: Dillon-Tyler, Publishers, 1975.

AZTEC RUINS NATIONAL MONUMENT, NEW MEXICO. John M. Corbett. Washington D.C.: National Park Service Historical Handbook, Series 36, 1962.

AZTEC RUIN, THE. E.H. Morris. Anthropological Papers of the American Museum of Natural History, vol. 27, part I. New York: 1919.

"BANDELIER NATIONAL MONUMENT, EXPLORATION," *Annual Bulletin of the School of American Research.* Albuquerque: Mcleod Printing Company, 1980.

BOOK OF THE HOPI. Frank Waters. New York: Ballantine Books, 1969.

CANYON DE CHELLY. Zorro A. Bradley. Washington, D.C.: National Park Service, Office of Publications, 1973.

EARLY MESOAMERICAN VILLAGES, THE. Kent V. Flannery. Albuquerque: Academic Press, 1976.

GILA CLIFF DWELLINGS. Elizabeth McFarland. Albuquerque: University of New Mexico Publications Office, 1967.

HANDBOOK OF NORTH AMERICAN INDIANS, SOUTHWEST, vol. 9. Washington, D.C.: Smithsonian Institution, 1979.

KIN KLETSO. Vivian Gordon and Tom W. Mathews. Globe, Arizona: Southwest Parks and Monuments Association, 1977.

LINDENMEIR: A PLEISTOCENE HUNTING SOCIETY. Edwin N. Wilmsen. New York: Harper and Row, 1974.

MESA VERDE. William C. Winkley. Cortez, Colorado: Interpark, 1977.

MESA VERDE, THE STORY OF. Gilbert R. Wenger. Mesa Verde Museum Association, Inc., 1980.

PREHISTORIC INDIANS OF THE SOUTHWEST. H.M. Wormington. Denver: Denver Museum of Natural History, 1947.

RECONSTRUCTING PREHISTORIC PUEBLO SOCIETIES. William A. Longacre. Albuquerque: University of New Mexico Press, 1970.

ROCK ART OF THE AMERICAN INDIAN. Campbell Grant. New York: Thomas Y. Crowell, 1967.

VOICES IN THE CANYON. Catherine W. Viele. Globe, Arizona: Southwest Parks and Monuments Association, 1980.

Index

ABO, 100–103. *See also* Salinas National
  Monument
Acoma Pueblo, 23
Anasazi, 8–10, 12, 19, 21, 23, 24; affect on
  Mogollon culture, 121; of Aztec, 81; of
  Canyon de Chelly, 90–93; of Chaco,
  95–98; of Comb Wash, 75, 76; of
  Coronado (Kuana Pueblo), 104–106; of
  Grand Gulch, 70–73; of Hovenweep,
  63–65; of Mancos Canyon, 86–88; of
  Mesa Verde, 82–85; of Monument
  Valley, 58–61; of Natural Bridges,
  66–69; Navajo National Monument, 49,
  51; of Pajarito Plateau, 112–118; of Pecos
  Valley, 108–111; of Salinas Valley, 101,
  103; of Salmon Ruins, 79; of Wupatki,
  45; Rainbow Bridge Trail, 52–55
Ancient Ones, 9, 10
Apache raiders, 103
Archaic Period, desert, 11, 18, 19, 27, 37
Astrological observations, primitive, 38,
  65, 98
Atlatl, 83
Aztec Indians, 20, 30
Aztec National Monument, 79–81

BALCONY HOUSE RUIN, 9, 84
Bandelier, Adolf, 115
Bandelier National Monument, 112–115,
  117
Bare Ladder Ruin, 67, 68
Basketmakers, 19, 49, 83, 91, 93
Betatakin Ruin, 8, 23, 49, 51
Bridges. *See* Natural Bridges National
  Monument, Rainbow Bridge Trail

Burials, Chaco Canyon, 97
Burial of the Hands, 92

CAJON RUIN, 63
Canals, use of: by Anasazi, 105, 115; by
  Hohokam, 27, 29, 37; by Sinagua, 29
Canyon de Chelly National Monument,
  8, 90–93
Canyon del Muerto. *See* Canyon de Chelly
Casa Chiquita Ruin, 97
Casa Grande Ruins, 36–38
Castles. *See* Cutthroat Castle, Hovenweep
  Castle, Montezuma Castle
Ceremonial Cave, 115
Chaco Culture National Historical Park,
  8, 22, 79, 81, 94–98
Cicuyé, 109–111. *See also* Pecos National
  Monument
Cliff Palace, 8, 84
Clovis Site, 18
Comb Wash, 74–76
Copper, use of, 21, 35, 37
Coprolites, 12
Cotton, use of, 20, 37, 84, 92, 105
Coronado, Francisco, 105, 109
Coronado State Monument, 104–106
Cummings, Byron, 55
Cutthroat Castle, 63
Cysts, storage, 70

DESERT ARCHAIC PERIOD. *See* Archaic
  Period
Digging Stick, 49
Dog, use of, 20, 49, 79, 83, 93

Dolores River, 8
Doorways: P shaped, 35; T shaped, 35

ESPEJO, ANTONIO, 30, 43

FAJADA BUTTE, 98
Folsom Site, 18
Foushee, Gene, 56
Frijoles Canyon, 113, 114

GILA CLIFF DWELLINGS NATIONAL
  Monument, 120–122
Gila River, 122
Gila Valley, 27, 30
Gila Wilderness, 121, 122
Gouldings Trading Post, 56, 59, 61
Gran Quivera, 101–103
Grand Gulch Primitive Area, 70–73

HACKBERRY RUINS, 63
Hand prints, Anasazi, 64
Hands, burial of. See Burial of the Hands
Historic Period, 13
Hohokam, 19, 21, 23, 27, 29, 30, 37, 38,
  43, 45, 121
Holly Ruin, 63
Homo sapiens, 17, 18
Hopi Indians, 23, 43, 51, 67, 92, 117
Horse Collar Ruin, 67–68
Horseshoe Ruins, 63
Hovenweep Castle, 63
Hovenweep National Monument, 62–65

ICE AGE, 17
Inca Indians, 20
Interglacial subages, 17

JACKSON, WILLIAM HENRY
  (photographer), 84
Jemez Pueblo, 109, 111

KEET SEEL RUINS, 8, 23, 49–51
Kidder, Alfred (archaeologist), 111

Kin Kletso Ruins, 94, 97, 98
Kino, Eusebio (padre), 37
Kiva, 67, 105, 106
Kuaua Murals, 106
Kuaua Pueblo. See Coronado State Park

LA PLATA MOUNTAINS, 8
Lomaki Ruins, 45, 46
Long House Ruins, 113, 115, 117

MANCOS CANYON, 23, 86–88
Mesa Verde National Park, 8, 23, 63, 79,
  81, 82–85, 87, 97
Mimbres, 121. See also Gila Cliff Dwell-
  ings National Monument, Mogollon
Mogollon, 19, 21, 23, 101, 103, 104–106,
  120–122
Montezuma Castle National Monument,
  28–31, 43
Montezuma Well, 28–31
Monument Canyon. See Canyon de Chelly
  National Monument
Monument Valley Tribal Park, 56, 58–61
Mormons, 65, 75
Mounds, platform, 27
Mummy Cave, 91
Murals, Kuaua. See Kuaua Murals
Mystery Valley, 59

NALAKIHU-CITADEL RUINS, 45, 46
Natural Bridges National Monument,
  66–69, 71
Navajo Mountain, 53, 55
Navajo National Monument, 9, 48–51
Nonnezoshi, 55

OÑATE, DON JUAN DE (governor of New
  Mexico), 103

PAJARITO PLATEAU, 113, 115, 117
Paleo-Indian Period, 11, 17–19
Pecos National Monument, 108–111
Penasco Blanco Ruins, 97

Petroglyphs, 23, 71; in Comb Wash, 75, 76, 101, 115
Phoenix Municipal Monument. *See* Pueblo Grande Ruin
Pictographs, 23, 71, 87, 115
Pima Indians, 23
Pithouses, 49, 83, 92, 95, 101, 121
Pithouse-Pueblo Period, 11, 19–21, 95, 101
Pleistocene Epoch, 17. *See also* Ice Age
Poc-ta-poc, 21, 46
Pottery, Anasazi, 69, 84, 92; Mogollon, 121; Sinagua, 43
Pueblo Alto, 97
Pueblo Bonito, 95, 96
Pueblo Grande Ruin, 27, 37
Pueblo Revolt, 109
Puye Ceremonial, 117
Puye Cliff Dwellings, 116–118

QUARAI, 100–103

RAINBOW BRIDGE NATIONAL MONUMENT, 52–55
Rainbow Bridge Trail, 52–55
Rattlesnakes, 55, 56, 72, 97
Recapture Lodge, 56, 59, 75
Ruins Canyon, 63

SALADO, 19, 21, 23, 33–35
Salinas National Monument, 100–103
Salmon, George (rancher), 79
Salmon Ruins, 78, 79, 81
Salt River Valley, 27
Sangre de Cristo Mountains, 109
San Juan County Research Center. *See* Salmon Ruins

Santa Clara Pueblo, 117, 118
Shoshone Raiders, 22, 23, 27, 37, 64, 67
Sinagua, 19, 21, 23, 29, 30, 41, 43, 45
Snake House Ruin, 74
Spruce Tree House Ruin, 84, 85
Square Tower Group Ruins, 63, 65
Subage, interglacial, 17
Surprise Valley (Utah), 53, 55

TARAHUMARA INDIANS, 117
Tobacco, use of, 27, 37, 105
Tonto National Monument, 32–35
Top House Ruin, 117, 118
Tsankawi Ruin, 113, 114, 117
Turkey, use of 20, 49, 71; use in blankets, 83, 93, 111
Tuzigoot National Monument, 42, 43
Tyuonyi Ruin, 113, 114, 117

UTE INDIANS, 22, 86–88
Ute Mountain Tribal Park, 86–88

VERDE VALLEY, 29, 30, 41, 43, 46

WALNUT CANYON NATIONAL MONUMENT, 40, 41, 46
Wattle and daub, 92
Wetherill, John, 55
Wetherill Mesa, 84
Wetherill, Richard, 8, 51, 85
White Canyon. *See* Natural Bridges National Monument
White House Ruin, 91–93; access to, 92
Wukoki Ruin, 45, 46
Wupatki National Monument, 23, 44–46

ZUNI PUEBLO, 23, 65